# Kent: A Birdwatcher's Site Guide

Chris Bradshaw and
Simon Busuttil

Shoebill

# Kent: A Birdwatcher's Site Guide

by Chris Bradshaw and Simon Busuttil

© Chris Bradshaw and Simon Busuttil
Published by Shoebill Books,  21 Giffords Way, Over,
Cambridge CB4 5UB

**ISBN** 0 9528065 2 5

Shoebill

Cover photographs by Tim Loseby

Line drawings by Will Woodrow

Printed by Crowes, Norwich, Norfolk

# Acknowledgements

This book would not be as accurate or as up-to-date if it were not for the assistance of a wide range of people.

We would particularly like to thank all landowners, site managers and reserve and country park staff for their helpful and often extensive comments on early drafts of the site accounts.

In addition, a number of birders made comments on the texts. In particular, we would like to thank John Cantelo and Andy Mckee for their extensive comments and suggestions which have improved the quality of the end product.

We would like to express our thanks to Richard Thomas, Phil Benstead and Steve Rowland for their help and advice during the preparation of this guide.

Chris would like to thank his wife Julie for her support and help with various aspects of the preparation of the site maps.

And finally, thanks to all those birders with whom we have spent time birding with in the county over the years.

# Contact us

We hope that *Kent: A Birdwatcher's Site Guide* will help you to get the most out of your birdwatching in this special county.

All of the sites in this book have been visited by the authors and the site managers consulted, but over time some details will inevitably change.

We would like to hear from you with any updates to the information presented here, and to receive information on sites not featured that might be suitable for inclusion in any future editions.

Please send your comments to:

Richard Thomas,
21 Giffords Way,
Over,
Cambridge CB4 5UB

Email shoebill.books@ntlworld.com

Thank you, and have a great time birdwatching in Kent...

# Contents

Key to map symbols ................................................................ vii

Introduction .......................................................................... 1

The Birdwatcher's Code of Conduct ......................................... 2

The Country Code .................................................................. 3

## Chapter 1  South-west Kent—Dungeness to Folkestone .. 4

Introduction .......................................................................... 4

1.01 Dungeness RSPB Reserve ............................................. 6

1.02 Dengemarsh ............................................................... 8

1.03 Dungeness Bird Observatory ...................................... 10

1.04 Dungeness - the Patch and seawatching ..................... 12

1.05 Greatstone Beach ...................................................... 14

1.06 Lade Pit ................................................................... 16

1.07 Scotney Pit ............................................................... 17

1.08 Walland Marsh .......................................................... 19

1.09 Copt Point ................................................................ 20

1.10 Folkestone Warren ..................................................... 22

1.11 Capel-le-Ferne ........................................................... 23

1.12 Samphire Hoe ........................................................... 24

## Chapter 2  East & north-east Kent Coastline ..................... 26

Introduction ........................................................................ 26

2.01 St Margaret's—South Foreland Valley to Dover ............ 29

2.02 Bockhill Farm and Kingsdown ................................... 31

2.03 Sandwich Bay Field Centre and Bird Observatory ......... 32

2.04 Pegwell Bay .............................................................. 34

2.05 North Foreland and Northdown Park ........................... 36

2.06 Minnis Bay ............................................................... 37

2.07 Reculver ................................................................... 39

2.08 Swalecliffe ................................................................ 41

## Chapter 3  Sheppey and the Swale Estuary ..................... 42

Introduction ........................................................................ 42

3.01 Elmley National Nature Reserve ................................. 44

3.02 Warden Point ............................................................ 46

3.03 Leysdown Coastal Park .............................................. 47

3.04 Swale National Nature Reserve .................................. 48

3.05 Capel Fleet and Harty Marshes .................................. 50

3.06 Oare Marshes Local Nature Reserve ........................... 51

3.07 South Swale Local Nature Reserve and Seasalter ......... 53

3.08 Conyer Creek ........................................................... 54

3.09 Murston ................................................................... 55

## Chapter 4 Thames and Medway Estuaries .......................... 58

Introduction ...................................................................58
4.01 Cliffe Pools ...........................................................60
4.02 Northward Hill.......................................................62
4.03 Allhallows and Yantlet Creek ................................64
4.04 Isle of Grain ........................................................65
4.05 Riverside Country Park ........................................67
4.06 Lower Halstow and Newington Cress Beds ...........68
4.07 Funton Creek .......................................................70
4.08 Trosley Country Park............................................71

## Chapter 5 Canterbury: The Blean and Stour Valley ........ 72

Introduction ...................................................................72
5.01 Stodmarsh National Nature Reserve ....................75
5.02 Grove Ferry .........................................................76
5.03 Westbere and Fordwich .......................................78
5.04 Seaton Pits and the Little Stour Valley ..................79
5.05 Blean Woods National Nature Reserve .................81
5.06 Thornden Wood....................................................82
5.07 East Blean National Nature Reserve ....................84
5.08 Larkeyvalley Wood ...............................................85
5.09 Park and West Woods, Lyminge Forest .................86
5.10 King's Wood, Challock .........................................87

## Chapter 6 Medway and the Weald .................................. 90

Introduction ...................................................................90
6.01 The Medway Valley ..............................................92
6.02 Mereworth and Hurst Woods ...............................94
6.03 Knole Park, Sevenoaks ........................................96
6.04 Sevenoaks Wildlife Reserve .................................97
6.05 Bough Beech Reservoir .......................................98
6.06 Tudeley Woods RSPB Reserve and Pembury Walks ............100
6.07 Bedgebury Forest and Pinetum ...........................102
6.08 Hemsted Forest....................................................103
6.09 Orlestone Forest/Faggs Wood .............................104
6.10 Hamstreet Woods ................................................106
6.11 Park or Great Heron Wood ..................................107

## Appendix 1 Kent checklist ............................................. 110

## Appendix 2 Useful addresses and contacts .................... 115

## Index ............................................................................ 117

# Key to map symbols

## Key

| | | | | |
|---|---|---|---|---|
| **CG** | coastguard station | | | hide |
| **i** | information | | | windmill |
| **P** | parking | | | viewpoint |
| **PH** | pub | | | church |
| **T** | telephone box | | | lighthouse |
| **VC** | visitor centre | | | golf course |
| **WC** | toilet | | | marsh/saltmarsh |
| **YC** | yacht club | | | orchard |
| campsite | | | broad-leaved woodland |
| hospital | | | coniferous woodland |
| cafe/restaurant | | | embankment/cliff |
| petrol station | | | |
| caravan park | | | track |
| picnic area | | | footpath |
| airfield | | | railway (with station) |
| surfaced road | | | |
| roundabout | | | |

coastguard station

information

parking

pub

telephone box

visitor centre

toilet

yacht club

campsite

hospital

cafe/restaurant

petrol station

caravan park

picnic area

airfield

surfaced road

roundabout

hide

windmill

viewpoint

church

lighthouse

golf course

marsh/saltmarsh

orchard

broad-leaved woodland

coniferous woodland

embankment/cliff

track

footpath

railway (with station)

## INTRODUCTION

Welcome to *Kent: A Birdwatcher's Site Guide*, the first comprehensive guide covering Kent, a county, which despite great pressures is still a very exciting place to go birdwatching. Both authors are birdwatchers with extensive knowledge of the county's birds. Simon Busuttil recently worked in Kent for many years as the RSPB reserves manager. Chris Bradshaw is a freelance ornithologist and birdwatching guide. We are both pleased to share our enthusiasm and knowledge with you.

The guide is designed to cover well known sites such as Dungeness and the Isle of Sheppey by breaking these into manageable chunks, but also many of the less well-known and smaller sites are included too. In all cases, the welfare of the birds has been put first and the wishes of the landowners and managers taken into account.

Most of the sites are managed in some way and many are nature reserves. The addresses of the organisations which run them are included at the back of the book. If you are not already a member of one or more of the organisations that protect birds and wild places in the county, then both authors urge you to join one of them. The Kent Ornithological Society (KOS) collates records of birds in the county and produces an Annual Report. These data are used by decision makers when planning the county's affairs so please submit your records to the county's recorders; relevant contact details are included at the back of the book.

Birdwatchers are ambassadors for conservation and most of what we do takes place in full view of the public eye. Please follow instructions for parking and access detailed in the book, and follow the Country Code and the Birdwatcher's Code of Conduct. This is increasingly important in a crowded county such as Kent where recently some of the best places were threatened with the construction of a huge airport, something that was fought by a coalition of local residents, birdwatchers and the professional conservation organisations. We must make sure our behaviour strengthens the pressure to protect birds and their habitats rather than weakens it.

Several businesses have advertised in this book. Please use them. Many are run by individuals who support conservation in some way. Please mention this guide if possible.

Shoebill

# The Birdwatcher's Code of Conduct

## 1 Welfare of birds must come first

Whether your particular interest is photography, ringing, sound recording, scientific study or just birdwatching, remember that the welfare of birds must always come first.

## 2 Habitat protection

A bird's habitat is vital to its survival, and therefore we must ensure that our activities do not cause damage.

## 3 Keep disturbance to a minimum

Birds' tolerance of disturbance varies between species and seasons. Therefore, it is safer to keep all disturbance to a minimum. No birds should be disturbed from the nest in case the opportunities for predators to take eggs or young are increased. In very cold weather, disturbance to birds may cause them to use vital energy at a time when food is difficult to find. Wildfowlers impose bans during cold weather: birdwatchers should exercise similar discretion.

## 4 Rare breeding birds

If you discover a rare breeding bird and feel that protection is necessary, inform the appropriate RSPB Regional Officer, or the Species Protection Department at The RSPB, The Lodge, Sandy, Beds SG19 2DL. Otherwise, it is best in almost all circumstances to keep the record strictly secret to avoid disturbance by other birdwatchers and attacks by egg-collectors. Never visit known sites of rare breeding birds unless they are adequately protected. Even your presence may give away the site to others and cause so many other visitors that the birds may fail to breed successfully. Disturbance at or near the nest of species listed on the First Schedule of the Wildlife and Countryside Act 1981 is a criminal offence.

## 5 Rare migrants

Rare migrants or vagrants must not be harassed. If you discover one, consider the circumstances carefully before telling anyone. Will an influx of birdwatchers disturb the bird or others in the area? Will the habitat be damaged? Will problems be caused with the landowner?

## 6 The law

The bird protection laws, as now embodied in the Wildlife and Countryside Act 1981, are the result of hard campaigning by previous generations of birdwatchers. As birdwatchers, we must abide by them at all times and not allow them to fall into disrepute.

## 7 Respect the rights of landowners

The wishes of landowners and occupiers of land must be respected. Do not enter land without permission. Comply with permit schemes. If you are leading a group, do give advance notice of the visit, even if a formal permit scheme is not in operation. Always obey the Country Code.

## 8 Respect the rights of other people

Have proper consideration for other birdwatchers. Try not to disrupt their activities or scare birds they are watching. There are many people who also use the countryside. Do not interfere with their activities and, if it seems that what they are doing is causing unnecessary disturbance to birds, do try to take a balanced view. Flushing gulls when walking a dog on the beach may do little harm, while the same dog might be a serious disturbance at a tern colony. When pointing this out to a non-birdwatcher, be courteous but firm. A non-birdwatcher's goodwill towards birds must not be destroyed by the attitude of birdwatchers.

## 9 Keeping records

Much of today's knowledge about birds is the result of meticulous record keeping by our predecessors. Make sure you help to add to tomorrow's knowledge by sending records to your county bird recorder.

## 10 Birdwatching abroad

Behave abroad as you would at home. This code should be firmly adhered to when abroad (whatever the local laws). Well behaved birdwatchers can be important ambassadors for bird protection.

### The Country Code

Enjoy the countryside and respect its life and work
Guard against all risk of fire. Fasten all gates
Keep your dog under close control
Keep to public paths across farmland
Use gates and stiles to cross fences, hedges and walls
Leave livestock, crops and machinery alone
Take your litter home. Help to keep all water clean
Protect wildlife, plants and trees
Take special care on country roads
Make no unnecessary noise

# Chapter 1 South-west Kent—Dungeness and Romney Marsh as far as Folkestone

## Introduction

The flat landscape of Romney Marsh was reclaimed from the sea and is enclosed by the former cliff line on top of which sit the ancient woods at Ham Street. To the west is the Weald of East Sussex and to the east, the chalk North Downs run into the English Channel ending in spectacular cliffs. Whilst the ancient wetlands have been long drained and converted to agricultural use, the activities of the aggregates industry have created hundreds of hectares of new wetlands in and around Dungeness. Many of these are now part of the RSPB Reserve and are managed for birds. They provide the focus for the wildlife interest of the area, which includes rare insects and plants as well as birds.

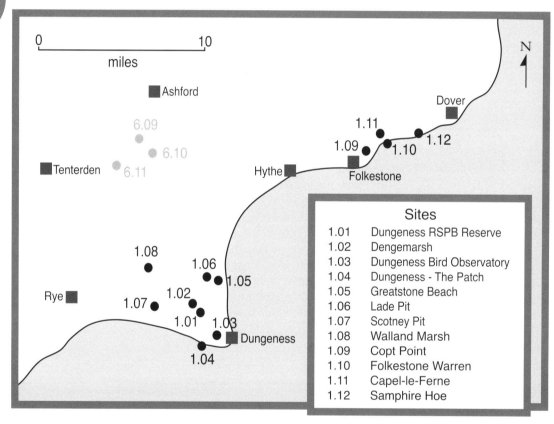

| Sites | |
|-------|---|
| 1.01 | Dungeness RSPB Reserve |
| 1.02 | Dengemarsh |
| 1.03 | Dungeness Bird Observatory |
| 1.04 | Dungeness - The Patch |
| 1.05 | Greatstone Beach |
| 1.06 | Lade Pit |
| 1.07 | Scotney Pit |
| 1.08 | Walland Marsh |
| 1.09 | Copt Point |
| 1.10 | Folkestone Warren |
| 1.11 | Capel-le-Ferne |
| 1.12 | Samphire Hoe |

**Map: Birdwatching sites in south-west Kent**

## Special birds

Dungeness and parts of the surrounding area are internationally important for wintering wildfowl including the largest flock of Bewick's Swans in Kent and one of the two regular flocks of White-fronted Geese in the county. Tens of thousands of waterfowl now winter in this area including one of the UK's largest populations of Smew, and the county's only regular Whooper Swans. Romney Marsh still supports reasonable numbers of farmland birds including Tree Sparrow and Corn Bunting. Habitat creation by the RSPB and others is encouraging reedbed birds, including Bittern and Bearded Tit, to winter and breed in increasing numbers. Offshore there is a regular passage of Pomarine Skuas in the spring, best seen from Dungeness, and a nationally important wintering flock of Sanderling at Lade Sands. At Copt Point, large numbers of Mediterranean Gulls gather during the winter. Protruding into the English Channel and close to the European mainland, Dungeness is a good place to experience migration. Whilst the large "falls" of migrants that occurred historically no longer happen regularly, there is always the chance of a rarity in the area, especially in spring. Species such as White Stork, Serin and Penduline Tit are regular visitors and there is an impressive list of other rarities for this area. North of Folkestone migration can be seen and heard along the cliffs and out at sea. This area has its special birds too–Peregrine occurs throughout the year and some scarce birds in Kent such as Shag and Purple Sandpiper are regular.

## Timing

A visit to this area can be worthwhile at any time of year although early July is often quiet. Between November and February there is a large number and variety of wintering birds, and in April/May, many migrants. Late July through to September is probably best for sheer variety, with gulls and terns (including Black, Roseate, and almost annual White-winged Black) offshore, waders on the wetlands, raptors such as Marsh Harrier and Hobby passing through, and the bushes and reedbeds full of migrating warblers. September and October can be excellent for migrants and the arrival of the first winter visitors.

## 1.01 Dungeness RSPB Reserve

A wild area of open shingle, scrub and wetland with a reputation for good birdwatching at most times of the year, but especially winter. This is one of the RSPB's "top twenty" reserves, and is a National Nature Reserve.

### Birds

Spring and autumn: migrants including waders, rarities
Summer: Hobby, Garganey, wildfowl, terns, Little Ringed Plover
Winter: wildfowl including Smew, the rarer grebes and divers, Bittern, Cetti's Warbler, Peregrine, Hen and Marsh Harriers.

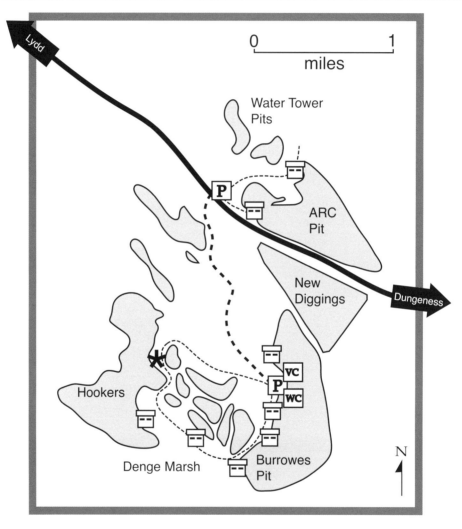

## Site 1.01 Dungeness RSPB Reserve

### Location (main entrance TR063197)

The main entrance to the reserve is located on the road between Dungeness and Lydd and is well signposted. The visitor centre is one mile down the track from here. A new car park opposite the main reserve entrance provides access to a nature trail, one hide and a viewing screen overlooking the ARC pit.

## Management

The RSPB's oldest reserve covers over 1,000 hectares of shingle and wetlands including reedbeds. The continuing maturation and creation of habitat make this an increasingly interesting place to visit.

## Opening times and access

The reserve, including the hides and viewing screens, is open between 09.00 and sunset every day of the year (except Christmas and Boxing Days). The visitor centre is open between 10.00 and 17.00 (March to October) and between 10.00 and 16.00 (November to February) except Xmas Day and Boxing Day when it is closed. Staff or volunteers are always on hand when the centre is open, to provide information. The visitor centre, toilets and most hides have provision for disabled visitors. Buses stop at the reserve entrance on request (except on Sundays).

## Other amenities

The RSPB shop in the visitor centre sells books, optical equipment and bird care products as well as tea, coffee and snacks.

7

## Birdwatching tips

The continual flow of migrants and variety of habitats make a visit interesting at any time of year. Hundreds of wintering wildfowl use the reserve and include Smew between late November and February, and the rarer grebes and divers are regularly seen. Bittern, Cetti's Warbler, Marsh Harrier, Bearded Tit and Water Rail can be seen at any time of year but are easiest in winter. In late summer Hobby and Marsh Harrier are present along with passage Black-necked Grebe, waders and warblers. Penduline Tit is recorded most years in October/November. Spring is best for migrants with raptors overhead, the rarer herons dropping in and the chance of a flyover migrant like a Golden Oriole!

Up-to-date information and a map can be obtained at the visitor centre. Walk the full nature trail concentrating on Burrowes Pit and the reedbed areas at Dengemarsh and Hookers, then visit the ARC pit, parking at the new car park opposite the main entrance to the reserve.

## Non-bird interest

In recent years both Lesser Emperor and Red-veined Darter dragonflies have been seen on the reserve and have probably bred. The nationally rare Jersey Cudweed is widespread and the lakes are full of Medicinal Leeches!

## 1.02 Dengemarsh

This is the only regular site for Whooper Swan in Kent, and sometimes attracts Bewick's Swan and wild geese. It is most easily watched from two public roads. Parts of the RSPB reserve can be viewed from Dengemarsh Road.

### Birds

Winter: Whooper and Bewick's Swans, geese, Merlin, harriers.

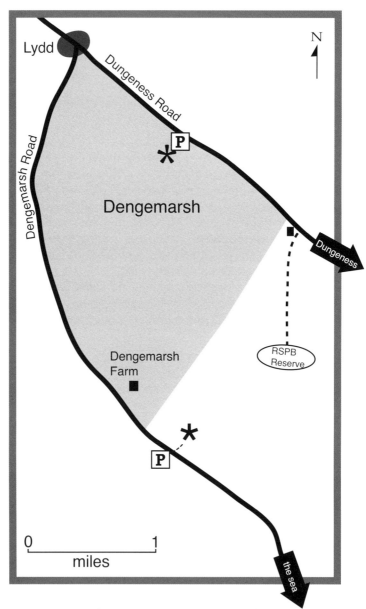

**Site 1.02 Dengemarsh**

### Location (centre of area TR053202)

This area of mainly arable fields lies north-west of Dungeness RSPB reserve (see 1.01), between the reserve and the village of Lydd.

## Management

These are arable fields. The swans feed mainly on oilseed rape.

## Opening times and access

Although public footpaths cross the area, it is recommended that the birds are viewed from the two public roads.

## Other amenities

There are shops, places to eat and public toilets in Lydd. There are also facilities at the RSPB reserve (site 1.01).

## Birdwatching tips

Whooper Swan is present between November and March. Some of the Walland Marsh flock of Bewick's Swans (see 1.08) can often be seen in this area too. The area is quite good for birds of prey such as Hen Harrier and Merlin. Scan in all directions.

Drive along the Dungeness Road between the RSPB reserve entrance and Lydd. The swans can be on either side of the road, usually half way between the reserve and Lydd where there is a good place to park off the road. At the roundabout in Lydd, turn left and then left again at the sharp right hand turning. This is Dengemarsh Road. Follow this dead end road as far as you need to. The swans will be on the north side of the road if they are present in this area. After Dengemarsh Farm, the area of wetland you can see on the left is part of the RSPB reserve. It is well worth scanning from the road. The road leads to the sea but the last mile or so is unmade and can be in poor condition. Watch out for migrants in the area.

## Note

Take great care along both roads.

## 1.03 Dungeness Bird Observatory

Jutting out into the English Channel, this flat stony area of bramble and willow is good for both migrating land and sea birds. Some of the area is a National Nature Reserve. In the shadow of the two nuclear power stations, Dungeness Bird Observatory carries out migration studies including ringing and seawatching. A warden is present throughout the year and up-to-date information on birds in the area can be obtained there. Dungeness has an excellent record of rarities.

### Birds

Spring and autumn: migrants, including rarities
Summer: Wheatear
Winter: Firecrest, Stonechat, Dartford Warbler.

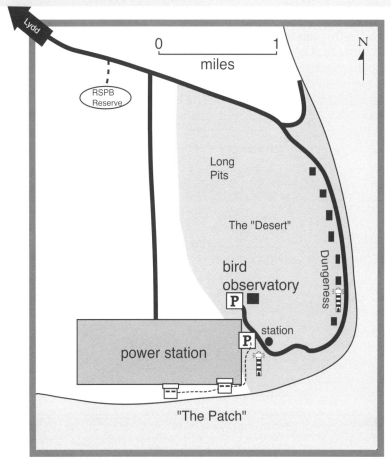

## Sites 1.03 and 1.04 Dungeness Bird Observatory and the Patch

### Location (bird observatory TR085173)

From Lydd, drive past the RSPB reserve and the road to the nuclear power stations on your right. Then turn right onto the private Dungeness Estate Road and drive past both lighthouses. At the power station fence there is a narrow tarmac road on your right with speed restriction signs and humps. Follow this to a terrace of "coastguard-type" houses partially hidden behind a high grass bank. The bird observatory is clearly signposted and is the closest house to the parking area.

## Opening times and access

This whole area is open to the public at all times, but please remember that people also live and work here. The bird observatory is open for most of the year and is wardened throughout. Buses stop on request on the Dungeness Road 1.5 miles away. A rather different way to visit is via the Romney, Hythe and Dymchurch Light Railway which runs irregularly throughout the year but mainly during school holidays.

## Other amenities

The bird observatory provides basic inexpensive accommodation for up to 10 people. Visitors need to bring their own sleeping bags, sheets and pillow cases. Call in advance to book 01797 321309. There is a cafe at the miniature railway station close by. Both the pubs at Dungeness serve food.

## Birdwatching tips

This is one of the few places in Kent where Wheatear regularly breeds. Look out for them among the houses. They can be seen from March through to October. Black Redstart nests on the power stations but is more common as a migrant in March and April and again in September and October. Firecrest, Chiffchaff and occasionally Dartford Warbler can be found in the scrub areas through the winter. Commoner migrants such as warblers, flycatchers and Redstart can be found in small numbers throughout the spring in the scrub and willows on the point. Serin is regularly recorded in spring. The best month for rarities is May. In recent years Black Stork, Black Kite, Audouin's Gull, Blyth's Reed and Sardinian Warblers have been recorded in this month.

After a midsummer lull, numbers of migrating land birds pick up again in September with large numbers of Swallows and martins passing overhead and small numbers of commoner migrants such as Pied Flycatcher and Redstart can be found in the bushes. Autumn rarities in recent years have included Pallid Swift, Short-toed Treecreeper, Isabelline Shrike, Pallas's and Dusky Warblers. In October, overhead visible migration can be exciting, with large numbers of finches and thrushes passing over. North-westerly winds and clear skies are the best conditions to observe this.

Birdwatching at Dungeness is unpredictable and weather conditions play an important part in watching birds here. For land birds, any wind with an easterly component can bring excitement, as do warm southerly winds in May. Rare birds can turn up at any time and anywhere!

## Non-bird interest

The observatory operates a moth trap on suitable nights of the year and is a great place to observe rare and migrant moths. Ask at the observatory for details. Other migrant insects including dragonflies and butterflies are often observed here.

## Note

The boundaries of private land are often not clear. Birds regularly turn up in people's gardens, so please respect resident's privacy.

## 1.04 Dungeness - the Patch and seawatching

Jutting out into the English Channel, this is a good place to observe sea birds and flocks of other species migrating over the sea. The warm water outflows from the power stations rise to the surface forming the so-called "Patch" that attracts large numbers of gulls, terns and other species to feed throughout the year. Information on birds and access to two hides can be obtained from the bird observatory (see 1.03).

### Birds

Spring: Pomarine Skua, Common Scoter, Sandwich and Black Terns
Summer: Manx and Balearic Shearwaters, Yellow-legged Gull, occasional Roseate Tern
Autumn: Sooty Shearwater, Arctic Tern, skuas, terns, occasional Sabine's Gull
Winter: auks, Red-throated Diver, Glaucous Gull, in recent years Caspian Gull has occasionally been seen.

### Location (car park TR089166) For map, see 1.03 above

Park next to the power station fence, or at the bird observatory (see 1.03). Walk along the power station fence towards the sea. Once on the beach, turn right and walk along the shingle bank. You will see the two hides ahead of you. The closer hide is generally used for seawatching whilst the second hide overlooks the Patch which lies just offshore.

### Opening times and access

This area is open to the public at all times. The bird observatory is open for most of the year and a key to gain access to their two hides can be obtained there. The use of the hides is not essential but they are a good place to seek shelter (and advice!). Buses stop on request on the Dungeness Road 1.5 miles away. A rather different way to visit is via the Romney, Hythe and Dymchurch Light Railway, which runs irregularly throughout the year but mainly during school holidays.

### Other amenities

The bird observatory provides basic inexpensive accommodation for up to 10 people. Visitors need to bring their own sleeping bags, sheets and pillow cases. Call in advance to book 01797 321309. There is a cafe at the miniature railway station close by. Both the pubs at Dungeness serve food.

### Birdwatching tips

Seawatching is generally best earlier in the day. Take the weather conditions into account when planning your visit - this is an exposed place. Throughout the winter, there are large flocks of Red-throated Divers, Great Crested Grebes and auks (mainly Guillemot) on the sea around the point. These are best observed in calm weather. Thousands of gulls are around the Patch at this time of year, including Kittiwake and occasional Iceland and Glaucous Gulls. Exceptional numbers of birds can be found when large numbers of sprats move inshore or during spells of cold weather. In early March, Dark-bellied Brent Geese move past the point, followed by Common Scoter and Sandwich Tern in early April. Common Tern and Bar-tailed Godwit move through in late April and early May, when the main event of the seawatching year at Dungeness takes place; small numbers of Pomarine Skua move past, often close inshore. Rarities in spring in recent years include White-billed Diver, Black-browed Albatross, Long-tailed Skua, Slender-billed and Bonaparte's Gulls. Onshore winds in June and July can bring Manx Shearwater inshore in small numbers often with Balearic Shearwater, which are becoming more commonly seen. Late summer interest often focuses on the seabirds around the point with Arctic, Black and other species of Terns and Yellow-legged and Little Gulls resting on the beach and feeding around the Patch. Poor weather conditions in late autumn can sometimes produce impressive numbers of seabirds including Sooty Shearwater and occasional Sabine's Gull or petrels.

12

Birdwatching at Dungeness is unpredictable and weather conditions play an important part in watching birds here. This is especially true of seawatching. Onshore winds are usually necessary to observe migrating birds offshore, especially in autumn and winter, and even then, occasionally nothing happens! In the spring, however, northward migration can often be observed in calm, even pleasant conditions! Calmer conditions are usually best to observe late summer gatherings of seabirds around the Patch or the large numbers of birds often present in late winter.

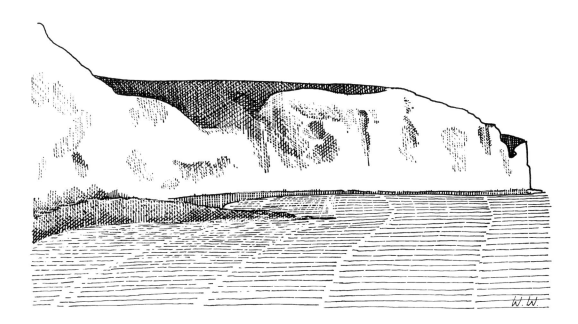

**Peregrine**

## 1.05 Greatstone Beach

Between Dungeness Point and Littlestone to the north is an area of silty sand exposed at low tide on the eastern shore of Dungeness. This can be productive at either high or better still, low tide at certain times of the year. The area is used heavily for recreation but can be good, especially in winter.

### Birds

Winter: Sanderling, Bar-tailed Godwit, Knot, Turnstone, gulls.

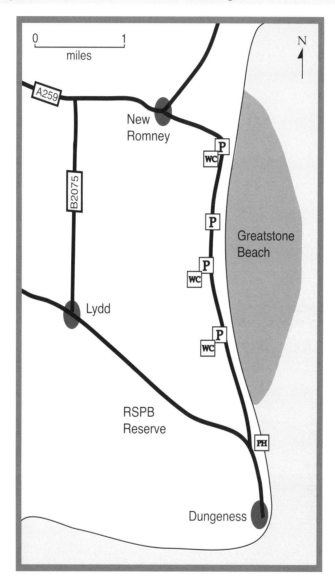

## Site 1.05 Greatstone Beach

**Location (car parks at TR085208, TR082219, TR083237 and TR081228)**

Park at one of the three, free public car parks along the coast road or at the fee-paying car park at TR083228. Then, either scan the shoreline or sea from just opposite the car park, or walk along the beach towards concentrations of birds. Mediterranean Gull can occasionally be seen at the southern car park. There are bus services along this route, which will stop on request.

## Opening times and access

There are no restrictions on access to the beach.

## Other amenities

There are shops and pubs along the coast road. Toilets are situated at two of the car parks but are often locked in winter.

## Birdwatching tips

This is always a pleasant spot to look for birds but is most productive during the winter months. There is a lot of disturbance to this area especially at weekends and almost continuously during the summer. Time your visit with the tides. At high tide small parties of waders roost on the beach, especially at the southern end, and birding is best on a rising or falling tide as the wading birds are closer in or fly by en route to their roosts. Waders are generally closer at the northern end of this beach where it is narrower. At low tide in winter, huge flocks of gulls are also present.

Sanderling is present between August and May, usually right by the water's edge. Other waders include Bar-tailed Godwit, Grey Plover, Oystercatcher, Curlew, Knot, Turnstone and Dunlin. The smaller species tend to roost on the shingle of Dungeness to the south whilst the larger species usually fly the short distance inland over the houses to the area around Lade Pit. Kentish Plover occasionally occurs here. In late winter, huge numbers of gulls sometimes congregate on the sands, making for an impressive spectacle at low tide. These can include Mediterranean Gull. At high tide, large numbers of Great Crested Grebe can be present in January. Gulls, terns and Gannet can be seen passing offshore at any time.

## 1.06 Lade Pit

Lade Pit is the nearest gravel pit to the sea on Dungeness. Whilst access is limited at present, it is currently being made part of the RSPB reserve and arrangements for viewing it are likely to change for the better in the near future. Birdwatching can be good at any time of year.

### Birds

Spring and autumn: migrants
Summer: wildfowl, grebes, terns
Winter: occasional Scaup, Smew, divers and rarer grebes, Bittern, gulls.

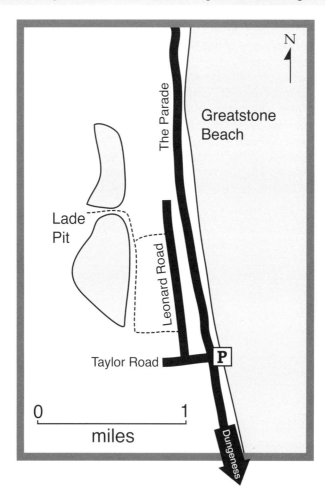

**Site 1.06 Lade Pit**

### Location (car park TR084208)

Lade Pit is just inland of the north-south running coast road (The Parade) on the eastern side of Dungeness at TR078214.

### Management

Lade Pit will soon be part of the RSPB Dungeness reserve.

### Opening times and access

Lade Pit is privately owned and still technically a working quarry but will soon become part of the RSPB reserve and access arrangements are likely to change in the next few years. Do not enter until signs and information tell you otherwise, or ask at the RSPB visitor centre

(Site 1.01). Please follow on-site signs and information. Park at the free car park on the coast road at TR084208 and walk from there.

## Other amenities
There are shops and pubs along the coast road. Toilets are situated at two of the car parks along this road but are often locked in winter.

## Birdwatching tips
Lade Pit is relatively undisturbed and can be productive for birdwatching at any time of year although autumn through to spring is best. The pit is used in winter by divers, the rarer grebes, Smew and Scaup. Bittern regularly occurs in winter and Dartford Warbler has been recorded in winter in the gorse scrub along the eastern side. Rarities in recent years have included Night Heron, Hoopoe, White-headed Duck and Canvasback.

## Warning
Lade Pit is privately owned and still technically a working quarry. The local primary school has requested that birdwatchers do not park outside the school.

**17**

## 1.07 Scotney Pit
This huge gravel pit lying on the border with East Sussex is well worth a visit, especially during the winter months when several thousand birds can be present.

### Birds
Year round: wildfowl, Corn Bunting, Barn Owl
Spring and autumn: migrants
Winter: White-fronted and Bean Geese, rarer grebes, divers, Scaup, Golden Plover, Little Stint, raptors including Hen and Marsh Harriers.

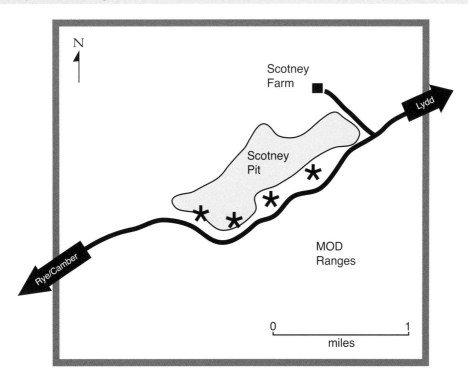

### Site 1.07 Scotney Pit

## Location (TR012194)
Scotney Pit lies on the East Sussex/Kent border along the Rye to Lydd Road.

## Management

Areas immediately to the east of Scotney are currently being worked and areas to the west and north will be worked in the future. The area and range of habitats will increase and improve over the next few years, and birdwatching is likely to get better.

## Opening times and access

Scotney Pit is best viewed from the public road and is therefore accessible at all times. Birdwatchers can park at several sites off the main road. National Cycle Route 2 runs along the south side of the pit and provides good birdwatching access by bicycle.

## Other amenities

There are shops and places to eat in both Lydd and Camber. There are daytime petrol stations at both too.

## Birdwatching tips

Scotney holds lots of birds throughout the year with breeding gulls, waterfowl and Lapwing through the summer, late-summer gatherings of Pochard and other ducks and good numbers of waterfowl during the winter. It is excellent for wildfowl including the rarer grebes and divers. One of only two flocks of White-fronted Geese regularly seen in Kent winter here between December and March. They can usually be seen on fields at the back of the gravel pit at its western end. Small numbers of other geese such as Bean Geese are sometimes with them. The flooded fields between the pit and the road often hold flocks of Lapwings and Golden Plovers and in winter Dunlin and occasionally Ruff and Little Stint. These fields can hold migrating waders in spring such as Dotterel. Corn Bunting and a few Tree Sparrow occur on the farm and can be seen throughout the year. Rarities have included Ring-necked Duck and Lesser Scaup.

## Warning

Take care parking along this fast dangerous road, and always pull well off the side.

**Mediterranean (foreground) and Black-headed Gulls**

18

## 1.08 Walland Marsh
This attractive area of arable and grassland behind Dungeness is easily accessible by car and better still by bicycle!

### Birds
Year round: Corn Bunting, Tree Sparrow, Barn and Little Owls
Spring: Yellow Wagtail, Whimbrel
Winter: Bewick's Swan, Hen and Marsh Harriers, Green Sandpiper.

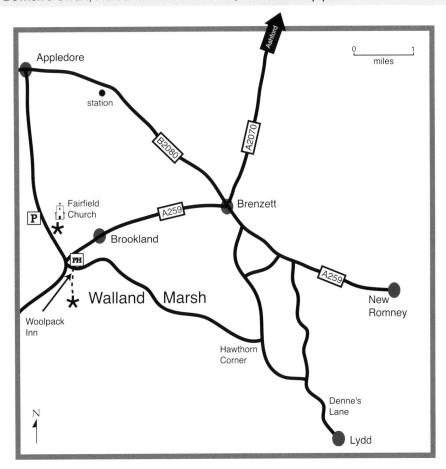

## Site 1.08 Walland Marsh

### Location (Brenzett TR007269)
The route referred to below covers the area between Lydd, Brookland, Appledore and Brenzett.

### Opening times and access
This area is accessible at all times by public road and footpath. National Cycle Route 2 runs through part of this area and links it to Site 1.07. Appledore Railway Station is on this route.

### Other amenities
There are some good pubs dotted across the marsh. There are shops and places to eat in Lydd and a petrol station at Brenzett.

## Birdwatching tips

There are still reasonable numbers of Corn Bunting and Tree Sparrow on Walland Marsh. In winter the largest herd of Bewick's Swans in the county feeds mainly on oilseed rape and there is a roost of Hen and Marsh Harriers.

Take this route on your way to, or from, other sites in the area such as Dungeness, or take your time and cover it by bicycle.

There is a heronry and large rookery in the trees around the Norman church at Lydd (TR043209). Between Lydd and the Woolpack Inn at Brookland, look out for Corn Bunting on the wires and fence posts and Tree Sparrow in older willows and around buildings. Look out for wet patches in fields which in spring can be especially good for flocks of Yellow Wagtail including Continental races. White Stork is now an almost annual visitor to the area in late summer and autumn. If around, Bewick's Swans may be seen on either side of this road. Opposite the Woolpack Inn at TQ978245 there is a footpath running south. After 300 yards it rises up on to a bank. To the left is an area of reed where on winter evenings Hen and Marsh Harriers roost. If you have not already seen the Bewick's Swans, they may be here. This is also a good place for Barn Owl at dusk.

The area around Fairfield Church is a small, attractive wetland area that in winter supports Wigeon and Teal and has regular Green Sandpiper, Little Egret and Hen and Marsh Harriers. It can be viewed from TQ965265 on the road running between Appledore and the Woolpack Inn.

Wet fields to the north of the B2080 on either side of the railway at Appledore Station are a traditional stopover site for Whimbrel in the spring. Stop at the railway station or turn off this busy road onto one of the minor roads. In spring, listen for Nightingale in any patch of scrub or wet woodland around Appledore.

Occasionally the herd of Bewick's Swans is close to Old Romney Village and can be seen from one of the minor routes off the A259, almost always to the south.

## Warning

Try to avoid cycling along the busy A259.

# 1.09 Copt Point

This area just north of Folkestone is the easiest place in Kent to see Mediterranean Gull at almost any time of year. A visit to this site can be easily combined with visits to sites 1.10, 1.11 and 1.12.

## Birds

Year round: Peregrine, Gannet, seabirds, Mediterranean Gull (best July-April)
Winter: Eider, Shag.

## Opening times and access

Accessible at all times from Wear Bay Road (parking is restricted here between April and September) or just off it, from the free public car park at TR240365 just below the coastguard lookout and next to the Pavilion pub. Folkestone Central railway station is 1 mile away. Buses pass close by and access by bicycle is easy; National Cycle Route 2 runs past this site.

## Other amenities

There are pubs and cafes nearby (some only open seasonally) and there are public toilets including disabled access (open Easter to Sept) at TR242371. There are plenty of places to eat in Folkestone (follow the signs to the harbour where there is a public car park).

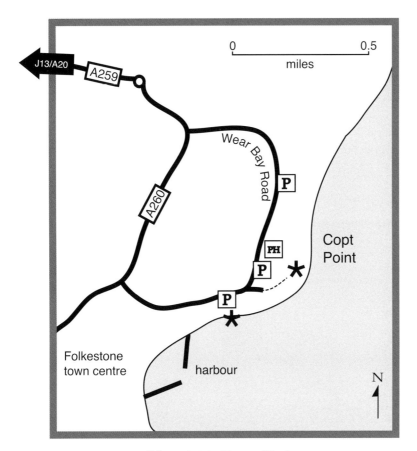

## Site 1.09 Copt Point

### Location (car parks TR240365, TR241366, TR241371)

Just north of Folkestone and overlooking the harbour. Parking is off Wear Bay Road. Approaching Folkestone from the A20 (junction 13), take the A259 and A260 following signs for the harbour and then the country park.

### Birdwatching tips

Once on Wear Bay Road look on the amenity grasslands (including the bowling club) between the road and the sea for Mediterranean Gull, which is often present in large numbers between July and March. A few are present between late April and June.

Also, check the roofs and chimneys of the houses on the opposite side of the road. Park in the car park at the Pavillion pub, and walk to the cliff edge. The path up to the coastguard lookout ends at a flat concrete area giving good views. Scan the rocks below to the left for roosting gulls including Mediterranean Gull and the sheltered bay below and in front of you for feeding gulls.

The bay and harbour provide shelter and often hold some interesting birds during the winter such as Eider, Red-breasted Merganser or occasionally Shag. At any time of year seabirds, such as terns and Gannet, can often be seen offshore and Peregrine can now be seen anywhere along this stretch of coast.

### Warning

The cliff edge is eroding and is dangerous. Heed all warning notices.

## 1.10 Folkestone Warren

Immediately north of Folkestone and Copt Point (Site 1.09) is The Warren, a fascinating area at the base of a slumped cliff providing sheltered areas of woodland, scrub and grassland between the chalk cliffs and the sea. An interesting variety of birds is present at any time of the year, and birdwatching is enlivened by the presence of the sea and by migration which can be very visible here. This is also one of the best places in Kent for Shag.

### Birds

Year round: Peregrine, Rock Pipit, Black Redstart, Stonechat, Fulmar, seabirds
Spring and autumn: migrants such as Wheatear, Firecrest, Ring Ouzel
Summer: warblers
Winter: Purple Sandpiper (now very scarce), Shag.

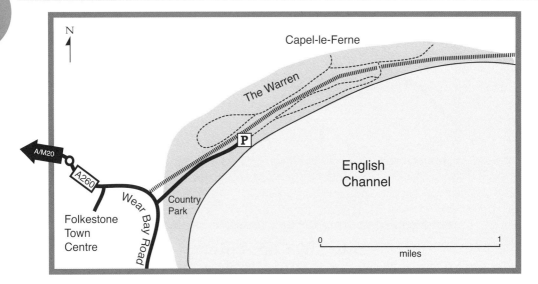

**Site 1.10 Folkstone Warren**

### Location

The Warren lies below Capel-le-Ferne (Site 1.11)

### Management

The Warren is a Local Nature Reserve and a Country Park and is managed by the White Cliffs Countryside Project (WCCP).

### Opening times and access

The Warren can be accessed from the Martello Tower at the top end of Wear Bay Road (for parking and directions, see Site 1.09) or by several paths from Capel-le-Ferne (see Site 1.11). A series of well-marked and managed footpaths, including the Four Seasons Nature Trail, give access to this area including the foreshore. Folkestone Central railway station is 1.5 miles away.

### Other amenities

There are seasonal cafes at The Warren, with others on the cliff-top at Capel-le-Ferne and pubs there and in nearby Folkestone. There are interpretation panels and a free leaflet is available from WCCP (01304 241806).

## Birdwatching tips

A visit at any time of year can be worthwhile. Explore the woodland and scrub for common birds and migrants. Scan the sky and cliffs above you for raptors and migrating birds and keep an eye out to sea for birds either on the water or passing offshore. For migrants a visit earlier in the day is recommended as the site can get busy. Follow the well-marked and managed paths (the Four Seasons nature trail) through the scrub to the concrete apron at the base of the cliffs. The scrub can be good for many species, including Firecrest during the winter. Once you are on the concrete apron at the base of the cliffs walk in either direction looking out to sea for seabirds and above you for Peregrine. Rock Pipit and Black Redstart can be seen at the base of the cliffs. A circular walk through the woodland and scrub and returning along the foreshore can be rewarding. Rarities include Greenish Warbler.

## Non-bird interest

The site is famous for its interesting plants such as Wild Cabbage and Rock Samphire.

23

## Warning

This area is subject to rock falls and landslips especially after rain; heed all warning notices. Occasionally paths are blocked. The concrete apron at the base of the cliff can be slippery when wet. Take extra care at high tide and in storms when waves break over the concrete apron.

## 1.11 Capel-le-Ferne

Capel-le-Ferne is the cliff-top section above Folkestone Warren (1.10). It provides exhilarating views out over the Warren and across the Channel to the French coast. It is a good place to watch out for migrants either moving overhead or in the scattered scrub.

### Birds

Year round: Peregrine
Spring and autumn: migrants.

## Management

There is management of the public rights of way.

## Opening times and access

Access via the public footpaths is possible at all times.

## Other amenities

There are seasonal cafes and pubs along the cliff-top.

## Birdwatching tips

Explore the scrub and fields. Look out for overhead migrants and watch for them out to sea also. Autumn is probably the best time. Rarities include Black Kite, Alpine Swift, Isabelline Wheatear and Olive-backed Pipit.

## Warning

Heed all warning signs. Much of the cliff-top is unfenced.

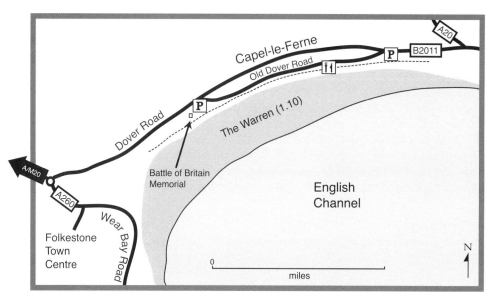

## Site 1.11 Capel-le-Ferne

### Location (area around TR250380)

Capel-le-Ferne is just north of Folkestone. Follow the signs for Capel-le-Ferne from the A20 or from Folkestone taking the B2011 and the Old Dover Road to access the cliff-top. There are several places to park along these two roads. All except the Battle of Britain Memorial car park (TR245382) are open at all times. The Memorial car park is free and open between 11.00 and 17.00 from 1 April to 30 September. The other places to park are lay-bys on the south side of the B2011 on either side of the entrance to the Memorial and along the Old Dover Road. Make your way to the footpaths along the cliff-top and explore. There are two footpaths down the cliff to link up with the walks described for 1.10 that add variety, but remember, you have to come back up!

### 1.12 Samphire Hoe

Samphire Hoe is an amazing place at the base of Shakespeare Cliff, created from the material excavated from the Channel Tunnel. The location gives stunning views of the white cliffs above and along the coast and it is easily accessible to all. Birds similar to those found at 1.11 are present at any time of the year. The newly created Hoe is gaining a reputation for migrants.

### Birds

Year round: Peregrine, Black Redstart, Stonechat, Fulmar, Rock Pipit, seabirds offshore
Spring and autumn: migrants such as Wheatear and Ring Ouzel
Summer: cliff-nesting House Martins.

### Management

Samphire Hoe is owned by Eurotunnel and managed in partnership with White Cliffs Countryside Project.

### Opening times and access

Samphire Hoe is open from 07.00 to dusk every day of the year. Access by car is only through a well-signposted tunnel from the A20 and there is a car parking charge.

On foot or by bicycle the Hoe is accessible from the cliff-top footpath (North Downs Way) and a cycle track (National Cycle Network Route 2) through the tunnel (entrance at TR300395). The site is accessible to all including wheelchairs and cycling is encouraged.

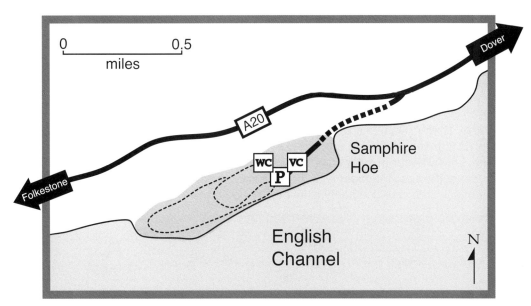

## Site 1.12 Samphire Hoe

### Location (access off A20 at TR300395)
At the base of the cliffs between Folkestone and Dover.

### Other amenities
There is an information centre and toilets (including disabled access), and a small cafe open most days from 10.00 to 15.00.

### Birdwatching tips
The site is heavily used so a visit earlier in the day is recommended. The friendly staff and volunteers at the information hut will provide information and there is a book of sightings. Watch offshore for seabirds either on the sea or passing by, explore the grassland areas via the network of paths for migrants, and keep looking above for Peregrine. Search the base of the cliffs for Black Redstart and Rock Pipit.

### Non-bird interest
There are chalk grassland plants including Early Spider Orchids. Insects include Red-veined Darter, Red-eyed Damselfly and Small Blue butterfly.

### Warning
Heed all warning signs.

## CHAPTER 2 East & north-east Kent Coastline

### Introduction

Kent's long coastline is one of the key reasons for the county's great attraction to birders, with the eastern part of the county being especially important for migrating birds. Much of the coastline is characterised by large tracts of coastal farmland, interspersed by the towns of Herne Bay, Thanet, Deal and Dover. Most of the northern coast is fairly low lying, but chalk cliffs rise up around Thanet and the Downs reach the sea between Deal and Folkestone. Low-lying areas of grassland exist around Sandwich, although much of this area is under golf course management. There is much to interest the birder at all times of the year, but this area is undoubtedly at its best during the autumn migration.

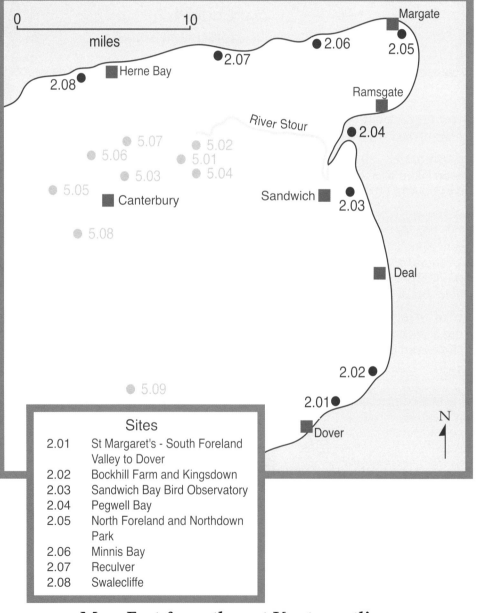

Sites

| | |
|---|---|
| 2.01 | St Margaret's - South Foreland Valley to Dover |
| 2.02 | Bockhill Farm and Kingsdown |
| 2.03 | Sandwich Bay Bird Observatory |
| 2.04 | Pegwell Bay |
| 2.05 | North Foreland and Northdown Park |
| 2.06 | Minnis Bay |
| 2.07 | Reculver |
| 2.08 | Swalecliffe |

**Map: East & north-east Kent coastline**

## Special birds

The area is important as a staging area for migrating birds. The entire coastline attracts good numbers of passerine migrants in both spring and, in particular, autumn. Scarcer species such as Ring Ouzel and Firecrest are recorded in small numbers throughout the area whilst rarer species such as Icterine Warbler, Yellow-browed Warbler, Pallas's Warbler, Red-breasted Flycatcher and Ortolan Bunting will almost certainly appear at one or more of these locations each year. Dotterel has become a regular autumn visitor to the St Margaret's area in recent years. This region has an excellent track record for rarities and most sites included here can be expected to turn-up a national rarity during the course of a year. Seawatching is excellent along the north coastline. Gannet, shearwaters, skuas, Little Gull, Kittiwake, terns and auks all occurring during suitable weather conditions.

Visible migration is often spectacular with good passages of hirundines, Skylark, pipits, wagtails and finches taking place in spring and autumn. These movements can involve tens of thousands of birds passing through during the course of a day or even a morning. Passage of raptors can be noticeable with the St Margaret's area probably getting as close to being a raptor bottleneck as anywhere in the UK. Osprey, Montagu's, Hen and Marsh Harriers, Sparrowhawk, Honey, Common and Rough-legged Buzzards, Hobby and Merlin are all regularly recorded each year whilst rarer species such as Red-footed Falcon and Black Kite are also reported sporadically.

Gulls are ever-present, but Mediterranean Gull and the scarcer Glaucous and Iceland Gulls are not infrequently recorded during the winter months.

Fulmar and Kittiwake breed on the chalk cliffs near Dover, whilst Peregrine has also re-colonised this area after an extended absence between the 1960s and1980s. Breeding Rock Pipits may be found at several locations in this part of the county, whilst Stonechat is also present.

## Timing

Birdwatching in this area is rewarding throughout the year, although most of these sites are at their best during migration periods, particularly during the autumn.

During the winter months there are small flocks of Snow Buntings and occasionally Shore Larks at several locations, whilst offshore there are usually large numbers of Red-throated Divers and auks. Seaduck, such as Eider and Common Scoter, may be present in sizeable numbers. The onset of freezing conditions usually initiates movements of wildfowl, Lapwing, Golden Plover, thrushes and other species fleeing cold weather in search of warmer climes further west.

Spring migration is not as productive a period as the autumn, but there are still notable movements of many migrant species. Visible migration is best observed during light winds from a westerly quarter, whilst south-easterly winds might produce arrivals of scarcer species. In late spring, fine conditions are conducive to arrivals of Honey Buzzards. Summer is the time to visit the colonies of Fulmars and Kittiwakes on the cliffs near Dover.

The autumn migration period is perhaps the most exciting time to visit the east Kent coastline. From mid August through to mid November, expect a wide variety of species as summer visitors depart for wintering quarters in conjunction with the arrival of winter visitors. August and September bring the main passage of chats, warblers and flycatchers with all the commoner species occurring regularly. Numbers of Whinchat, Redstart and Pied Flycatcher are heavily influenced by the incidence of easterly winds, but you might be considered unlucky should a visit to this part of the county at this time of year fail to produce at least one or two of these species. Scarcer species such as Ring Ouzel and Firecrest can be expected in late September and October, with small numbers frequently recorded in March/April. Seawatching is good along the north coast during winds from a northerly quarter, and sizeable skua movements can take place at anytime between mid August and mid November, with Arctics dominating the August/September period and Great Skua becoming more common from mid September onwards. Pomarine Skua may occur at any time, but is more likely to be encountered during October. North-west winds may also produce a variety of raptor species, with St Margaret's and North Foreland in particular regularly recording small movements including Common Buzzard, Sparrowhawk, Hen and Marsh Harriers, Merlin, Short-eared Owl and, more rarely, Rough-legged Buzzard, Montagu's Harrier, Osprey and Honey Buzzard.

**Pallas's Warbler**

## 2.01 St Margaret's—South Foreland Valley to Dover

Situated on the south side of St Margaret's village, this area of chalk grassland with scrub and woodland is attractive to migrant passerines and is one of the best migrant traps in the county. The cliffs between here and Dover support breeding Fulmar, Kittiwake and Peregrine.

### Birds

Spring: migrant raptors (including Honey Buzzard), passerine migrants
Summer: Fulmar, Peregrine, Kittiwake, Rock Pipit, Stonechat
Autumn: Dotterel, migrant raptors, passerine migrants including Firecrest, Ring Ouzel, scarce and rare migrants.

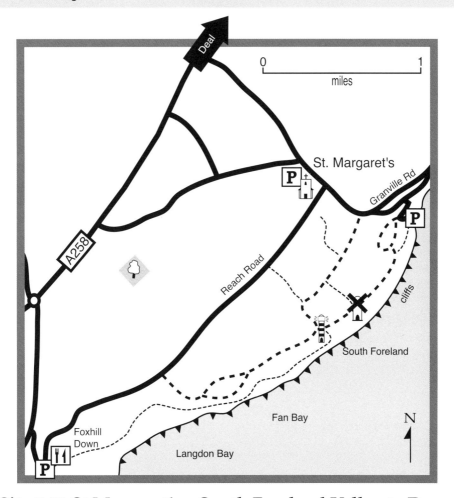

## Site 2.01 St Margaret's—South Foreland Valley to Dover

### Location (main car park TR368445)

From St Margaret's village follow the road down to the beach and park. From here walk south-west into the valley. There are further car parks in St Margaret's village and a National Trust car park at Langdon Bay can be reached by driving along Reach Road in the direction of Dover (free to National Trust members).

## Management

Part of the area is owned by the National Trust. Much of the South Foreland valley is owned by St Margaret's-at-Cliffe Parish Council, and is being managed with the assistance of White Cliffs Countryside Project (WCCP). There are interpretation panels and a free leaflet about the Heritage Coast available from WCCP (01304 241806).

## Opening times and access

There is public access at all times.

## Other amenities

There is a cafe and toilets at the National Trust car park near Langdon Bay. All amenities can be found in the village of St Margaret's or in nearby Dover.

## Birdwatching tips

The area is at its best during migration periods. Winds from an easterly quarter are likely to be most productive for grounded migrants. Explore the South Foreland valley early in the morning since many birds move quickly through the area and do not linger. Check the cliff-top fields for Dotterel in the second half of August and first half of September. Visible migration, which can be watched from the cliff-top near the lighthouse, is likely to be most productive during north-west winds. The area is good for raptor migration during spring and autumn when Marsh and Hen Harriers, Sparrowhawk, Common Buzzard and Merlin are all recorded. Honey Buzzard is regular in May/June and September. The small wood by the lighthouse regularly attracts Yellow-browed and Pallas's Warblers in late October and early November. Rarities are regularly found and in recent years European Bee-eater, Booted, Sardinian, Greenish, Radde's and Dusky Warblers and Little Bunting have all been recorded. Stonechat can be found breeding in the gorse near Langdon Bay, where there are colonies of breeding Kittiwake, Fulmar and usually Peregrine.

## Warning

The cliffs along this section of coast are high and prone to occasional rock falls. Do not approach the cliff edge too closely.

## 2.02 Bockhill Farm and Kingsdown

An area of coastal farmland and scrub with a golf course on the tops of the chalk cliffs north of Dover. One of the best migrant traps in the county, this site is especially good in the autumn. A superb visible migration watchpoint.

### Birds

Spring: migrant raptors (including Honey Buzzard), passerine migrants
Summer: Fulmar, Kittiwake, Rock Pipit
Autumn: migrant raptors, passerine migrants including Ring Ouzel, Grasshopper Warbler, Firecrest, scarce and rare migrants.

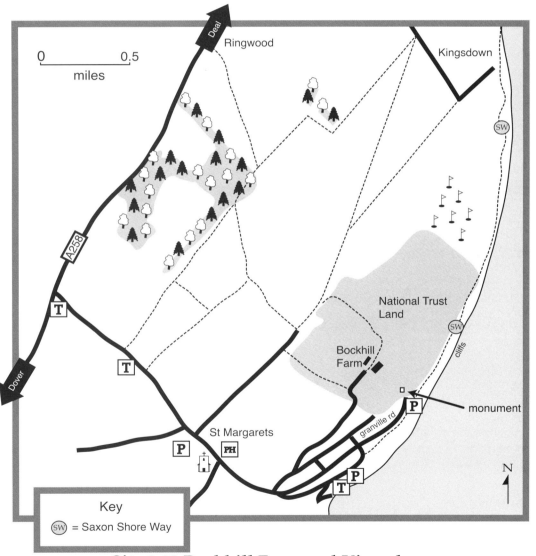

## Site 2.02 Bockhill Farm and Kingsdown

### Location (main car park TR374452)

From St Margaret's village take Granville Road and follow to the car park near the monument.

## Management

Part of the area is owned by the National Trust.

## Opening times and access

There is access along public footpaths at all times. Do not enter the golf course and respect local residents' privacy when birding around gardens.

## Other amenities

All amenities can be found in the village of St Margaret's or in nearby Dover. There are cafes in the beach car park and on the cliff top by the monument. Toilets are located in the beach car park, but are often locked outside the tourist season.

## Birdwatching tips

The area is at its best during migration periods. Anywhere can produce interesting birds, but be sure to check the trees and scrub around Bockhill Farm and work the cliff-top scrub along the coast to Kingsdown. Falls of continental migrants are most likely during periods of easterly winds. Visible migration watches from the monument at Bockhill are likely to be most productive during north-west winds. Scarce species such as Pallas's and Yellow-browed Warblers and Ortolan Bunting have been regular in recent years, whilst the site has a growing reputation for producing some outstanding rarities with Red-rumped Swallow, Red-flanked Bluetail, Nutcracker, Radde's and Booted Warblers and Alpine Accentor all recorded in recent years. Although not ideal for seawatching, divers, shearwaters, skuas and terns may be observed from the beach.

## Warning

The cliffs along this section of coast are high and prone to occasional rock falls. Do not approach the cliff edge too closely.

## 2.03 Sandwich Bay Field Centre and Bird Observatory

Sandwich is home to one of Kent's two bird observatories. Situated at the mouth of the River Stour this extensive area of farmland, golf courses, gardens and scrub is attractive to a wide variety of migrant species. Recent management work undertaken by the Sandwich Bay Bird Observatory Trust has further enhanced the area with the creation of wader scrapes.

## Birds

Year round: Eider, Corn Bunting
Spring: Marsh Harrier, Kentish Plover, terns, migrant passerines, scarce and rare species
Summer: terns
Autumn: waders (including Little Stint, Curlew Sandpiper, Wood Sandpiper), chats, warblers, flycatchers, finches, scarce and rare species
Winter: Lapwing, Golden Plover, Jack Snipe, Twite, Lapland Bunting, Snow Bunting.

## Management

The Sandwich Bay Bird Observatory Trust and Kent Wildlife Trust manage large parts of the area.

## Opening times and access

A toll road allows vehicles access to the observatory and much of the Sandwich Bay Estate, however, ensure that you keep to public rights of way.

## Other amenities

There is self-catering accommodation with shared cooking and washing facilities for up to 18 people at the visitor centre. In addition there is a self-contained flat that sleeps two. All amenities can be found in the nearby town of Sandwich.

32

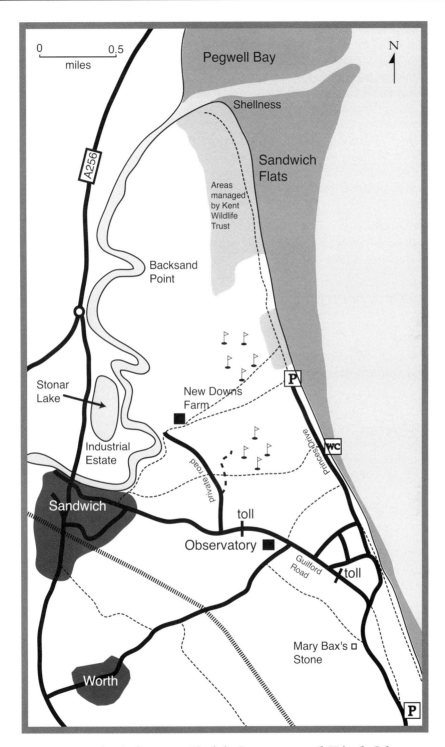

# Site 2.03 Sandwich Bay Field Centre and Bird Observatory

**Location (main car park TR356575)**

From Sandwich take the minor road east towards the Sandwich Bay estate. After 1.5 miles you will reach the tollgate where a fee to access the estate roads is payable. Drive a further 0.5 miles to reach the observatory.

## Birdwatching tips

This area is excellent for migrants of all kinds. Autumn is best with the most interesting birding likely to be associated with periods of easterly or south-easterly winds when a wide variety of commoner passerine migrants can be expected. Pallas's and Yellow-browed Warblers are regular in October and early November. The area has a fine reputation for rarer species, which in recent years have included Black Kite, Red-footed Falcon, Sharp-tailed Sandpiper, Alpine Swift, Isabelline and Lesser Grey Shrikes, Icterine, Sardinian, Radde's and Dusky Warblers, Red-breasted Flycatcher and Little Bunting. Members of Sandwich Bay Bird Observatory Trust may visit Backsand scrape for waders. The new observation tower at the observatory affords excellent views over the surrounding area and is a great place to observe visible migration. Ask at the observatory for details of the most recent sightings.

## Non-bird interest

There is a wide variety of orchid species at the site and these are best seen during May through July. The area is also good for moths.

## Note

Please respect the privacy of local residents on this private estate.

## 2.04 Pegwell Bay

Pegwell Bay is a large bay formed where the River Stour reaches the sea. An excellent area for wildfowl and waders, the scrub around the car park is also attractive to migrants.

## Birds

Spring: Kentish Plover and other passage waders, terns
Summer: Roseate Tern
Autumn: waders (including Curlew Sandpiper, Greenshank)
Winter: Dark-bellied Brent Goose, Golden Plover and other waders, gulls.

## Management

Kent County Council and Kent Wildlife Trust are responsible for the management of the area.

## Opening times and access

There is access to the area on foot at all times. Please pay attention to the car park closing times that are displayed at the entrance.

## Other amenities

There are nearby petrol stations both north and south of the car park. There is a toilet block at the car park. Car park costs 20p per hour, 50p per day except Sunday when the rates are 30p and £1 respectively. All amenities can be found in the nearby towns of Ramsgate or Sandwich.

## Birdwatching tips

Best visited 2-3 hours before high tide when the rising waters force waders close to the shore. Early morning is the best time to search for migrants since the area is popular with dog walkers. This is one of the best places in the county for Kentish Plover, which sometimes appears during periods of south-east winds in spring and autumn. There have been regular records of Roseate Tern in July and August in recent years. A telescope is very useful at this site as the birds are often distant.

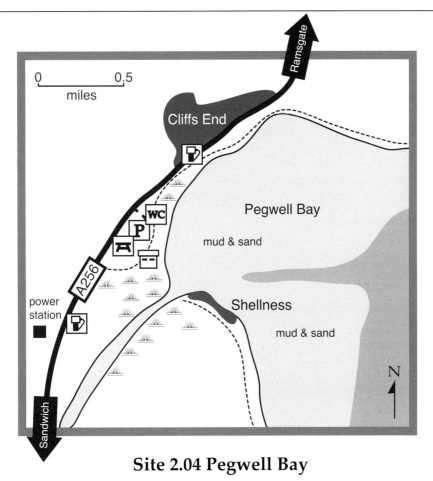

**Site 2.04 Pegwell Bay**

## Location (car park TR342633)

From Ramsgate follow the A256 south towards Sandwich. The car park is on the east side of the road just south of Cliffs End village. Bus services between Ramsgate and Sandwich pass the entrance to the car park.

## 2.05 North Foreland and Northdown Park

An area of rough grassland and cliff-top scrub bordered by gardens and golf courses. Northdown Park is a large open space with large trees that are attractive to migrants and is perhaps the best-known site in Kent for Rose-ringed Parakeet.

### Birds

Year round: Fulmar, Rose-ringed Parakeet, Black Redstart, Rock Pipit
Spring: migrant raptors, passerine migrants
Autumn: Gannet, shearwaters, raptors, skuas, auks, Redstart, Ring Ouzel, Pied Flycatcher, Icterine, Yellow-browed and Pallas's Warblers
Winter: Red-throated Diver, Eider, Common Scoter, Sanderling, Purple Sandpiper, auks.

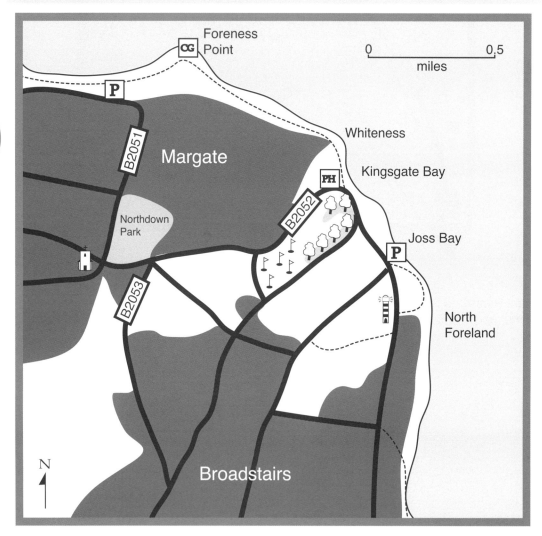

### Site 2.05 North Foreland and Northdown Park

### Location (Joss Bay car park TR399700)

From Margate follow the coastal B2051 to Foreness Point where you can park at TR380714. Northdown Park is reached by travelling half a mile south from Foreness Point where you can park on the road (TR378703). North Foreland is reached by taking the B2052 east and then south to reach the lighthouse or by driving north from Broadstairs.

## Opening times and access
There is access along public footpaths and minor roads at all times. Do not enter the golf courses and respect the privacy of local residents when birding around gardens.

## Other amenities
All amenities can be found in Margate or Broadstairs.

## Birdwatching tips
Foreness Point and North Foreland are both excellent for seawatching in winds from a northerly or easterly quarter. Strong northerly winds in late October or November are likely to produce movements of Little Auk. Any area of rough grass, fields or scrub is worth checking for migrant passerines. North-west winds can trigger movements of raptors such as Common Buzzard, Sparrowhawk and occasionally Rough-legged Buzzard. The area has produced regular records of both Richard's and Tawny Pipits, although these have been less frequent in recent years. Pallas's and Yellow-browed Warblers are scarce but regular visitors in September-November. Rare species have included Pied Wheatear, Booted, Dusky and Radde's Warblers, Collared Flycatcher, Isabelline Shrike and Rustic Bunting. Rose-ringed Parakeet can be found easily in Northdown Park. Purple Sandpiper and Sanderling roost at high tide in the Whiteness area.

## Warning
The cliffs along this section of coast are high and prone to occasional rock falls. Do not approach the cliff edge too closely.

## 2.06 Minnis Bay
The eastern half of an area of coastal farmland between the towns of Herne Bay and Birchington. This area is most productive during migration periods, in particular the autumn when large numbers of migrants may be present.

### Birds
Spring: returning summer migrants, Marsh Harrier, Hobby, Ring Ouzel
Autumn: Gannet, Manx and Sooty Shearwaters, skuas, Little Gull, auks, migrant warblers, chats, flycatchers
Winter: Red-throated Diver, Great Crested Grebe, Eider, auks, Snow Bunting.

## Opening times and access
There is public access at all times.

## Other amenities
All amenities can be found in Birchington.

## Birdwatching tips
Walk west along the seafront to reach the stables where the scrub often attracts interesting species. Continue west along the counter wall, cross over the railway and follow the footpath SSW to Shuart Farm, which is an excellent area for migrant passerines. The path leading to the farm is excellent for thrushes during October with Ring Ouzel often encountered. Yellow-browed Warbler is regular around the farm in September and October. The path running east towards Hale can also be productive. Retracing your steps to the railway, you can continue west along the railway embankment to Chamber's Wall where you can walk north to Coldharbour Lagoon and then return eastwards along the seawall to reach Minnis Bay. Seawatching can be good from one of the shelters on the low cliffs at Minnis Bay. The whole area has the potential for turning up rare species, with Squacco Heron, Surf Scoter, White-winged Black Tern, Desert Wheatear, Greenish and Bonelli's Warblers and Woodchat Shrike amongst the rarer species recorded in recent years.

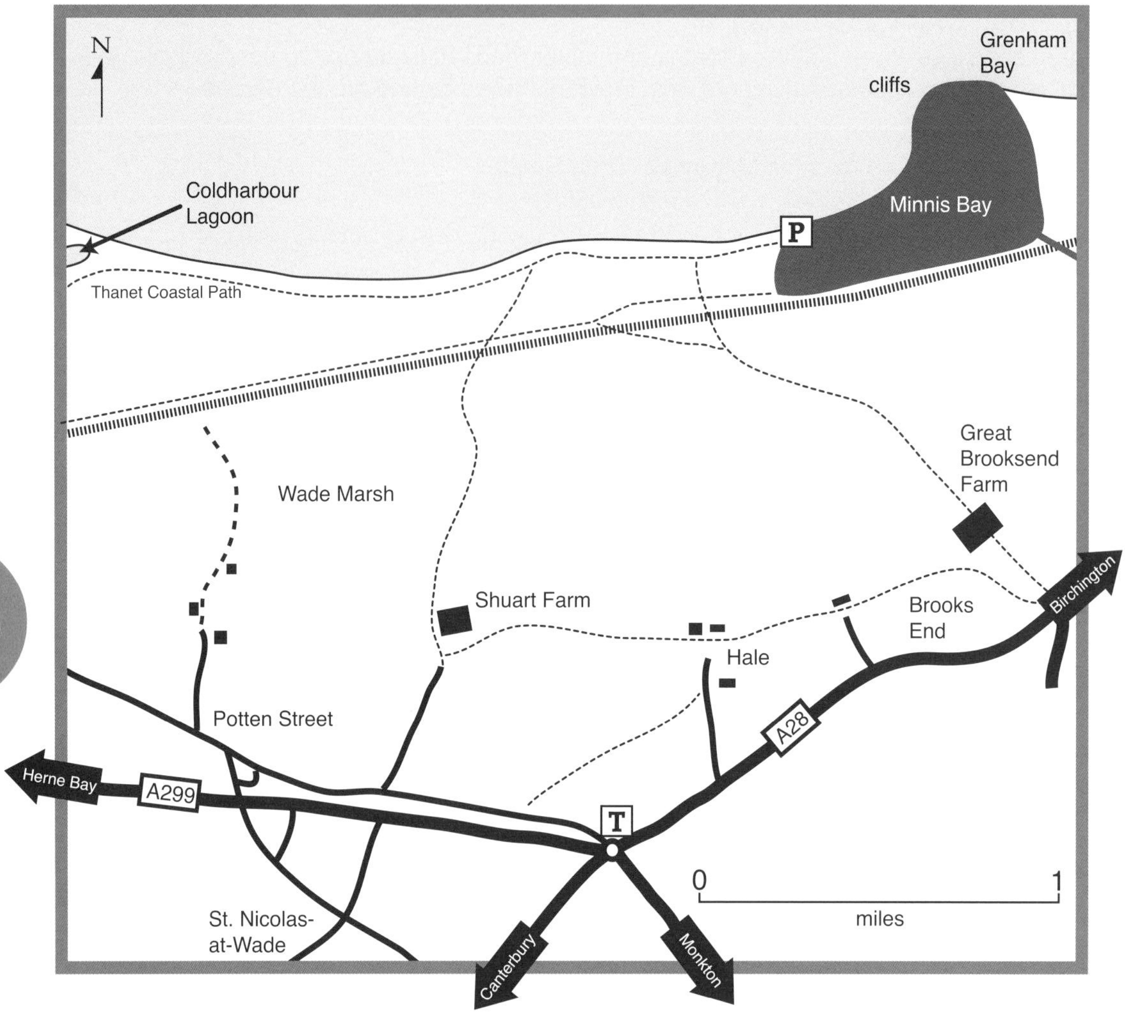

N

Grenham
Bay

cliffs

Coldharbour
Lagoon

Minnis Bay

P

Thanet Coastal Path

Great
Brooksend
Farm

Wade Marsh

Shuart Farm

Brooks
End

Birchington

Hale

38

A28

Potten Street

Herne Bay

A299

St. Nicolas-
at-Wade

T

0                                    1

miles

Canterbury

Monkton

## Site 2.06 Minnis Bay

### Location (car park TR285694)

From the A28 turn north into Birchington and follow the road to Minnis Bay. Park on the seafront at Minnis Bay and walk westwards to explore the area. Alternatively, take the minor road that parallels the A299 west off the A28/A299 roundabout east of St Nicholas-at-Wade. Turn north to reach Shuart Farm where there is limited parking.

## 2.07 Reculver

The western half of the area of coastal farmland between the towns of Herne Bay and Birchington. This area is most productive during migration periods, in particular the autumn when large numbers of migrants may be present.

### Birds

Spring: returning summer migrants, Marsh Harrier, Hobby, Ring Ouzel
Autumn: Gannet, Manx and Sooty Shearwaters, skuas, Little Gull, auks, migrant warblers, chats, flycatchers, Lapland Bunting
Winter: Red-throated Diver, Great Crested Grebe, Dark-bellied Brent Goose, Eider, auks, Shore Lark, Snow Bunting.

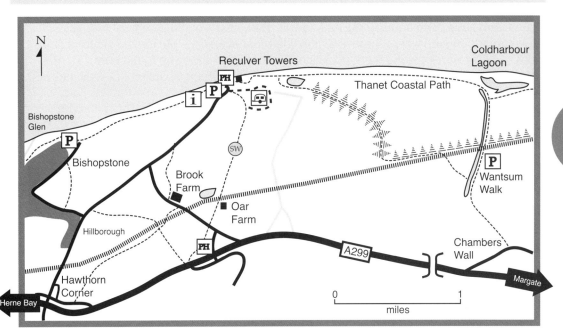

### Site 2.07 Reculver

### Location (car park TR226693)

Bishopstone Glen: from the A299 take the minor road north at Hawthorn Corner following signs to Beltinge/Reculver. At Hillborough turn left and then first right to reach the car park at Bishopstone.

Reculver Towers: from the A299 take the minor road north at Hawthorn Corner following signs to Beltinge/Reculver. Turn right at Hillborough and follow the road to Reculver Towers.

Chambers Wall: from the A299, take the minor road north-east, approximately 3 miles east of Hawthorn Corner. Take the track on the left and follow to the fisherman's car park. Alternatively, follow directions to Shuart Farm (see Site 2.06) but follow the minor road westwards through Potten Street to the track to the fisherman's car park.

### Opening times and access

There is public access at all times.

### Other amenities

There is an information centre and toilets, and several small convenience stores and cafes close to Reculver Towers. All other amenities may be found in nearby Herne Bay.

## Birdwatching tips

From the Bishopstone car park walk west along the coast and into Bishopstone Glen to search for migrants. Explore any and all of the minor roads and footpaths that pass through fields and scrub attractive to migrants. This is a particularly good area for migrant warblers and flycatchers and has hosted Yellow-browed, Dusky, Greenish, Arctic and Barred Warblers and Red-breasted Flycatcher.

Watch visible migration or seawatch from Reculver Towers. Visible migration is most productive in light west or north-west winds. Seabirds will pass during winds from a northerly quarter in the autumn, when impressive movements of skuas (including Pomarine and Long-tailed), shearwaters, auks and sometimes a few petrels may take place. The bushes surrounding the nearby caravan park have hosted Wryneck, Icterine, Subalpine, Yellow-browed, Hume's and Greenish Warblers in the past, whilst Pied and Desert Wheatears have been seen along the seawall. Walk east along the seawall to reach Coldharbour Lagoon where there is a high tide roost of waders. During the winter a small flock of Snow Buntings and more occasionally Shore Larks may be found here.

Another good area is to park in the fisherman's car park at Chambers Wall and walk north to reach the Coldharbour Lagoon. The ditches in this area have attracted Purple Heron in the past, whilst the fields and scrub around the car park and railway line are attractive to migrants. Scarce species recorded include Red-breasted Flycatcher, Woodchat Shrike and Ortolan Bunting. In the winter months a flock of Dark-bellied Brent Geese is usually present in the area.

## Warning

The cliffs between Bishopstone and Reculver are unstable and prone to occasional cliff falls. Therefore the cliff edge should not be approached too closely.

**Pomarine Skua chasing terns**

## 2.08 Swalecliffe

An area of rough coastal ground and scrub that is attractive to migrants.

### Birds
Autumn: passerine migrants
Winter: Red-throated Diver, Great Crested Grebe, Snow Bunting.

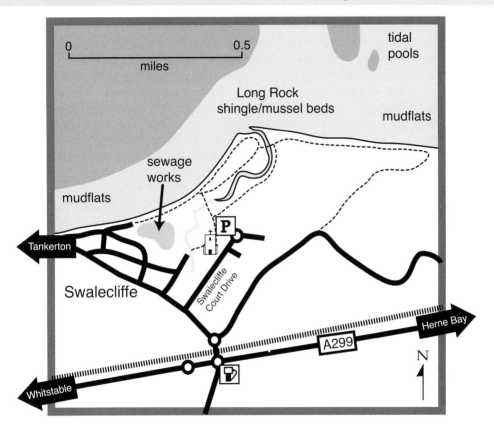

**Site 2.08 Swalecliffe**

### Location (car park TR136673)
From the A299, turn north into Swalecliffe. Take Swalecliffe Court Drive and park on the road near the church.

### Opening times and access
There is public access at all times.

### Other amenities
All amenities can be found in Tankerton.

### Birdwatching tips
Explore the scrub for migrants in spring and autumn. Snow Bunting is regularly recorded on the shingle during late autumn and winter. Seabirds may be seen offshore, although there are better watchpoints nearby (e.g. Reculver). An early morning visit is preferable since this site is very popular with dog walkers. Scarce migrants have included Richard's Pipit, Icterine and Yellow-browed Warblers, Red-backed Shrike and Common Rosefinch.

## CHAPTER 3 | Sheppey and the Swale Estuary

### Introduction

The Swale estuary is a large tidal channel that separates the Isle of Sheppey from the Kentish mainland. The Swale supports internationally important numbers of wildfowl and waders during the winter and migration periods. The southern side of the Isle of Sheppey is characterised by reclaimed fresh marshes and arable farmland, although some of this arable land is now being returned to grazing. This particular area is of exceptional wildlife interest with National Nature Reserves at both Elmley, which includes a portion managed by the RSPB, and The Swale. The northern side of the island rises to a high point of 180 feet around Warden Point, which is a reliable location for migrant passerines. The western portion is more heavily built up and is, on the whole, much less interesting for birdwatching. The south side of the Swale is similar in character to the southern side of Sheppey, with large areas of reclaimed fresh marsh. However, areas of arable farmland and orchards encroach upon the marshland, much reducing its expanse. There are excellent Kent Wildlife Trust reserves at both Oare Marshes and South Swale that protect some of the most important areas.

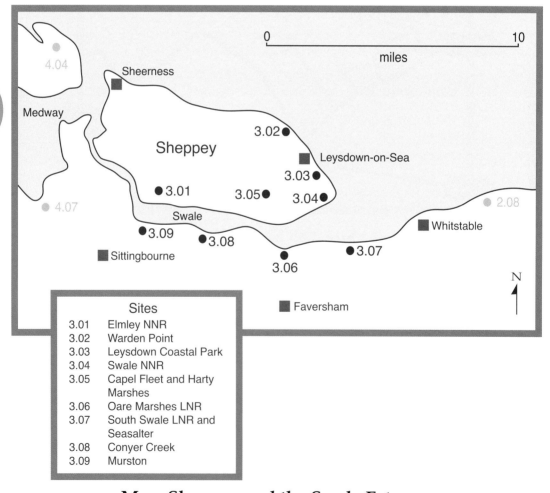

| Sites | |
|---|---|
| 3.01 | Elmley NNR |
| 3.02 | Warden Point |
| 3.03 | Leysdown Coastal Park |
| 3.04 | Swale NNR |
| 3.05 | Capel Fleet and Harty Marshes |
| 3.06 | Oare Marshes LNR |
| 3.07 | South Swale LNR and Seasalter |
| 3.08 | Conyer Creek |
| 3.09 | Murston |

**Map: Sheppey and the Swale Estuary**

## Special birds

The whole area is internationally important for wintering wildfowl and waders. Sheppey hosts the largest flock of wintering White-fronted Geese to be found in the county. The concentrations of wildfowl and waders are a spectacle hard to beat anywhere in the county, and virtually all of Kent's regular wintering ducks and waders can be found in considerable numbers. Breeding waders include excellent populations of Avocet, Lapwing and Redshank. Passage waders such as Spotted Redshank, Greenshank, Ruff, Common and Green Sandpipers all occur in good numbers during spring and autumn, whilst this area regularly records the largest numbers of Curlew Sandpipers and Little Stints in the county. Rare waders appear on an annual basis. This is by far the best area for raptors in the county and probably in south-east England, with good concentrations of Marsh and Hen Harriers, Merlin and Peregrine recorded mainly throughout the winter months, whilst Hobby is an increasingly common species during the summer. Scarce species such as Rough-legged Buzzard, Osprey and Montagu's Harrier are regular visitors, whilst almost all of the rare raptor species on the Kent list have appeared at some time or other on the Isle of Sheppey. The area supports significant populations of wintering Short-eared Owl, whilst Barn and Little Owls are also well represented. There is a regular passage of skuas and other seabirds during the autumn.

## Timing

Birdwatching in this area is excellent throughout the year. Late February sees the first signs of spring with a build up of Black-tailed Godwits, generally reaching a peak by late March when Wheatear, Sand Martin and Garganey will all have appeared. During April, breeding activity amongst waders such as Redshank, Lapwing and Oystercatcher is in evidence whilst passage waders include Ruff, Common Sandpiper and Spotted Redshank. Mediterranean Gull can frequently be found feeding in fields with flocks of Black-headed Gulls at this time. During May, a wide selection of waders pass through and most of the breeding species will have arrived. There is an excellent chance of finding a rare migrant.

43

During the summer Avocet breeds at most of the reserves, whilst the large colonies of gulls, and lesser numbers of Common and Little Terns, are also a feature.

Signs of autumn migration are noticeable as early as mid June when the first Spotted Redshank and Green Sandpiper appear. However, it is not until mid July when the autumn wader migration is fully underway and a wider selection of species appear. Numbers and variety remain relatively high throughout August and the first half of September. September and October are excellent periods for searching out interesting passerine migrants with the possibility of something more unusual such as Wryneck, Red-backed Shrike or Yellow-browed Warbler whilst reedbeds in the area often resound to the 'pinging' of erupting Bearded Tits.

Seabird passage commences in late August and continues well into December during periods of northerly/easterly winds. All four skuas are regularly seen and movements of Gannet, terns, Kittiwake, divers and auks can, at times, be spectacular. For those with enough patience, prolonged watches can bring scarcer species such as Sabine's Gull, Leach's Petrel, Little Auk and occasionally Sooty Shearwater.

Winter sees the highest concentrations of wintering wildfowl and waders present in the area. The presence of raptors will be much in evidence on the Isle of Sheppey. Flocks of Snow Buntings and perhaps Lapland Bunting and Shore Lark may be found in the eastern part of the Swale, whilst offshore large numbers of grebes and divers are likely to be present.

## 3.01 Elmley National Nature Reserve

A large area of lowland wet grassland managed as a RSPB and National Nature Reserve. It supports huge numbers of waterfowl during the winter months and is home to important populations of migrant and breeding waders. The site records rarities in most years and is probably the best site in Kent for rare waders.

### Birds

Year round: Marsh Harrier, Peregrine, Little and Barn Owls
Spring: Spoonbill, Garganey, Black-tailed Godwit, Whimbrel, Spotted Redshank, Ruff
Summer: Hobby, Avocet, Mediterranean Gull, Yellow Wagtail
Autumn: Spoonbill, passage waders (including Curlew Sandpiper, Little Stint)
Winter: Bewick's Swan, White-fronted Goose, ducks, waders, Hen Harrier, Merlin, Short-eared Owl, Twite.

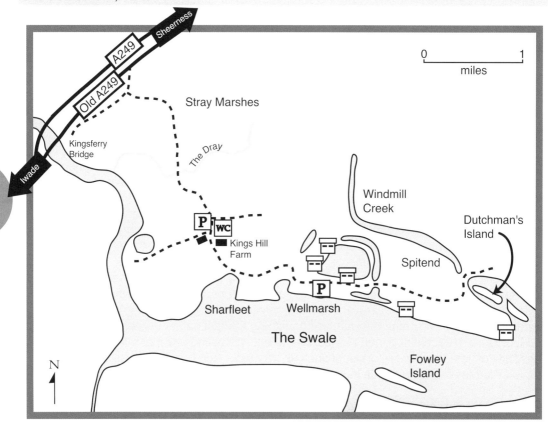

44

## Site 3.01 Elmley National Nature Reserve

### Location (main car park TQ938679)

The reserve is signposted (though easily missed) off the old A249 to Sheerness on the Isle of Sheppey, 1 mile beyond the old Kingsferry Bridge (do not take the new bridge and dual carriageway as there is no exit onto the reserve track). It is a further 2 miles along a rough track to the main car park.

### Management

Managed by the RSPB and as a National Nature Reserve.

## Opening times and access

The reserve is open daily (except Tuesday), 09.00 to 21.00 or sunset when earlier. There are five hides, the nearest of which is 1.25 miles from the car park, whilst the furthest (Spitend Hide) is a 6.5 mile round trip. There are toilets at the car park at Kings Hill farm. Special access arrangements can be made for the disabled and elderly, who may make use of the Wellmarsh car park.

## Other amenities

There is a garage at nearby Queenborough. Shops and most other amenities may also be found in Queenborough or nearby Sheerness. A fast food outlet is located on the A249 just north of the junction with the A2 before reaching the island.

## Birdwatching tips

The reserve is worth visiting at any time of year. A winter visit is recommended to see spectacular numbers of wildfowl and waders, whilst autumn wader passage is best between late July and early October. Timing your visit to coincide with high tide will maximise your chances of seeing large numbers of roosting waders. The track between the main road and Kings Hill farm is worth a careful look, particularly around The Dray. Please avoid getting out of your car here as it will cause disturbance. There is an information board detailing recent sightings in the car park at Kings Hill farm. Search the oak trees around Kings Hill farm for Little Owl. Scan the counter walls for harriers cruising along in search of prey. Peregrines sometimes perch on the fence posts at the rear of the flood. The long walk to Spitend Hide will reward with good views of the breeding colony of gulls including Mediterranean. Twite has been erratic in recent years, but might be found during the winter at Spitend. Spoonbill is regularly recorded, especially during spring and early autumn. A long list of rarities includes Black Stork, American Wigeon, White-tailed Eagle, Pallid Harrier, American and Pacific Golden Plovers, White-rumped, Baird's, Sharp-tailed and Semipalmated Sandpipers, Greater and Lesser Yellowlegs, Bonaparte's Gull and Great Reed Warbler.

## Non-bird interest

Hares and Foxes are frequently seen around the reserve. The site is regionally important for Water Voles. Scarce Emerald Damselfly has recently colonised and is worth looking for amongst the more common Emerald Damselflies. Other than a one-off record on the Hoo Peninsula, Elmley Marshes is the only site that the large, spectacular "Maid of Kent" beetle is known to occur in the UK. Look out for this species buzzing around cow pats in hot weather.

**Little Egret**

## 3.02 Warden Point

An area of caravan parks and cliff-top fields with scrub and small areas of woodland that are attractive to migrants in spring and especially autumn.

### Birds

Spring and autumn: migrant passerines, including chats, warblers and flycatchers.

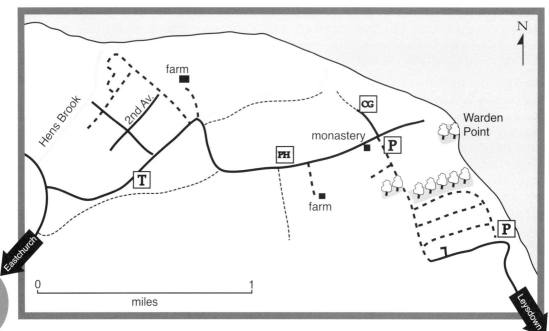

## Site 3.02 Warden Point

### Location (main car park TR016723)

Turn north by the church in the centre of the village of Eastchurch. Turn right after 0.5 miles and follow the road for 2 miles. Park in the open area near the monastery and explore the adjacent area to search for migrants.

### Opening times and access

There is open access at all times.

### Other amenities

The nearest garage is in Eastchurch. Shops and other amenities are located in Eastchurch or Leysdown. Several of the caravan parks host small convenience stores.

### Birdwatching tips

The area is worth a visit at migration times. Light winds from a southerly direction are most productive in spring, whilst winds from an easterly quarter are best during the autumn. The trees around the monastery hold most interest, with regular arrivals of warblers, flycatchers and Goldcrest. Firecrest is noted in small numbers most years, whilst there are regular autumn records of both Yellow-browed and Pallas's Warblers, with scarce species such as Icterine Warbler, Red-breasted Flycatcher, Red-backed Shrike and Serin all recorded in recent years. During periods of light winds from a westerly quarter visible migration can be interesting for hirundines, pipits, wagtails and finches.

### Warning

Whilst not particularly steep, the cliffs along the north coast of Sheppey are unstable and dangerous and should not be approached too closely. On no account attempt to scale them!

## 3.03 Leysdown Coastal Park

An area of coastal scrub and rough grass south of Leysdown which attracts migrants during spring and especially autumn. Extensive mudflats provide feeding areas for waders and gulls. Seawatching can be productive in suitable weather conditions.

### Birds

Year round: waders, Marsh Harrier
Spring: chats, warblers
Autumn: Gannet, Manx Shearwater, Common Scoter, Eider, skuas, Little Gull, Black Tern, chats, warblers and flycatchers
Winter: Red-throated Diver, Great Crested Grebe, Hen Harrier, Merlin, Peregrine.

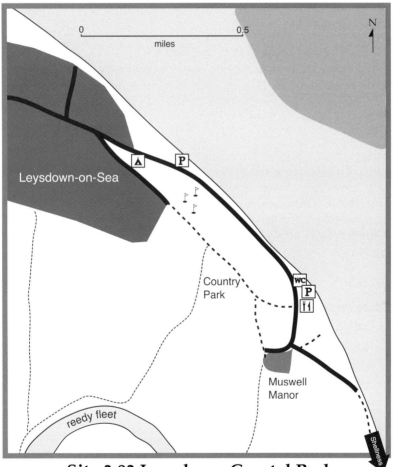

## Site 3.03 Leysdown Coastal Park

### Location (main car park TR044697)

The coastal park is immediately south of Leysdown. Take the minor road leading south of the town and park at the car park by the cafe and toilet block (often locked).

### Management

Local authority country park.

### Opening times and access

There is open access at all times along public footpaths. This site is especially suitable for those with mobility problems since many species can be observed from a vehicle.

## Other amenities

A small cafe by the car park serves drinks and snacks during the summer months. There are several phone boxes in Leysdown, where all other amenities, including a garage, cafes and toilets, can be found.

## Birdwatching tips

Explore the scrub and rough grassland searching for migrants. Winds from an easterly quarter are most likely to produce arrivals of passerine migrants with a good chance of rare or scarce species. There are several records of Wryneck during late August or September. Autumn seawatching is most productive during winds from a northerly or easterly quarter. Flocks of gulls on the grassy areas regularly hold Mediterranean Gull. Scan the fields to the west for raptors. An early start is recommended since the area suffers from disturbance by dog walkers.

## 3.04 Swale National Nature Reserve

An English Nature managed area of grazing marsh with shallow floods, saltmarsh and a shell beach with extensive mudflats, supporting large numbers of wintering and passage wildfowl and waders. The site offers some of the best seawatching in Kent during suitable weather conditions.

### Birds

Year round: waders, Marsh Harrier, Corn Bunting
Spring: Garganey, Curlew Sandpiper, Little Stint
Summer: Avocet, Little Tern, Yellow Wagtail
Autumn: Gannet, Manx Shearwater, Leach's Petrel, seaduck, Dotterel, skuas, Little Gull, Black Tern, chats, warblers and flycatchers
Winter: Red-throated Diver, Great Crested Grebe, White-fronted and Dark-bellied Brent Geese, Golden Plover, Snow and Lapland Buntings.

### Management

An English Nature managed National Nature Reserve.

### Opening times and access

There is open access at all times along public footpaths.

### Other amenities

There are several phone boxes in Leysdown, where all other amenities, including a garage, cafes and toilets, can be found.

### Birdwatching tips

Autumn seawatching is most productive during winds from a northerly or easterly quarter. The scrub in the car park at Shellness is productive for passerine migrants whilst the ditch system may be worth checking for Aquatic Warbler during August. Dotterel sometimes appear in the fields here (May or August/September). Winds from the south-west in August and September will sometimes result in substantial arrivals of passage waders, especially Bar-tailed Godwit, Whimbrel, Greenshank, Little Stint and Curlew Sandpiper. During the winter months Snow Bunting is regularly seen on the shell beach. Occasional parties of Shore Larks are noted there during November and December in most years. Lapland Bunting may occur anywhere in the area, but has become scarce in recent winters, as has Twite. Flocks of White-fronted Geese regularly visit the flooded grazing marsh in the evening. There is a regular harrier roost on the saltmarsh during the winter months. Rare species have included Red-breasted Goose, Black-winged Stilt, Oriental and Black-winged Pratincoles, Broad-billed and Terek Sandpipers and White-winged Black Tern.

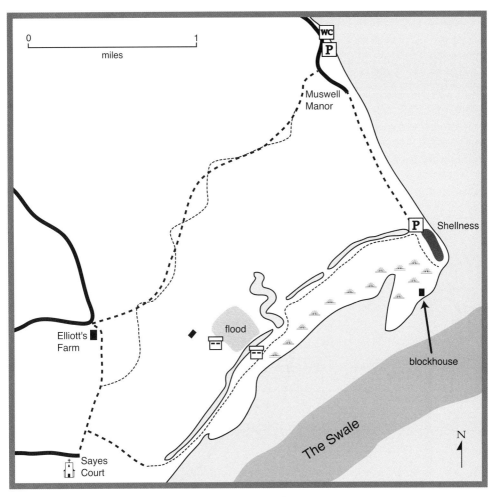

## Site 3.04 Swale National Nature Reserve

### Location (Shellness car park TR051681)

From Leysdown take the minor road south past Leysdown Coastal Park (site 3.03). Follow the road to the left at Muswell Manor and continue south-eastwards to the hamlet of Shellness along a very rough track. Alternatively, you can park at Leysdown Coastal Park (TR044697) and walk south from there.

### Warning

Note that the path to Shellness regularly floods at high tide. On no account should you walk along or within the protective counter wall along the western flank of the small hamlet at Shellness. Access along the shore of the hamlet is restricted to the area below the mean high water mark.

49

## 3.05 Capel Fleet and Harty Marshes

An area of farmland with reedy ditches and fleets especially attractive to birds of prey throughout the year.

### Birds

Year round: Marsh Harrier, Peregrine, Grey and Red-legged Partridges, Lapwing, Barn Owl, Corn Bunting
Spring: Garganey, Avocet, Mediterranean Gull
Summer: Hobby, Avocet, Mediterranean Gull, Yellow Wagtail
Autumn: Montagu's and Hen Harriers, Merlin, Hobby, Whinchat
Winter: Bewick's Swan, White-fronted Goose, Hen Harrier, Merlin, Golden Plover, Lapwing, Ruff, Short-eared Owl, Stonechat, Lapland Bunting.

50

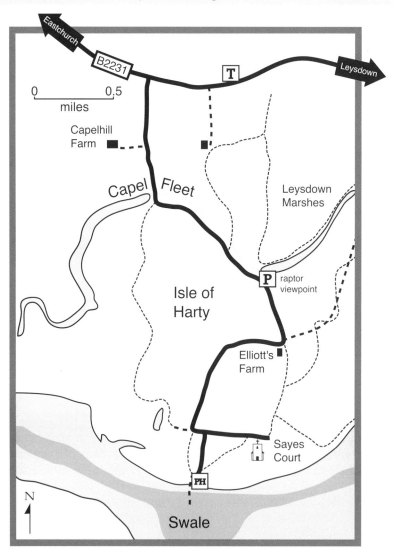

## Site 3.05 Capel Fleet and Harty Marshes

### Location (Capel Fleet TR010690)

From the B2231 Eastchurch to Leysdown road turn south on the minor road signposted to Harty Ferry Inn.

## Opening times and access
There is open access at all times along the Harty Ferry road and public footpaths. Please use the car park at the raptor viewpoint. Where possible, avoid parking in passing places along this narrow road.

## Other amenities
The Harty Ferry Inn offers food and drink with fine views over the Swale estuary. All other amenities can be found in nearby Eastchurch and Leysdown.

## Birdwatching tips
Drive the Harty Ferry road stopping regularly to scan. The site is at its best in winter when good numbers of birds of prey (sometimes including Rough-legged Buzzard) are present, but the area is excellent for raptors throughout the year. Marsh Harrier is present all year round, whilst Montagu's Harrier is recorded in most years during July and August. Winter flocks of White-fronted Geese are present between December and early March, with the largest numbers after Christmas, but are often distant. Check Capel Fleet for Mediterranean Gull, especially during spring and summer. Continue to Harty Ferry Inn where there are excellent views over the Swale and a regular roost of waders. Little Egret is frequent on the saltmarsh here and Avocet may be found breeding. Recent rarities have included White-tailed Eagle, Red-footed Falcon, Crane and Black-headed Bunting.

## 3.06 Oare Marshes Local Nature Reserve
A Kent Wildlife Trust reserve comprising wet grassland, shallow floods and reedbeds. Affords good views of the Swale Estuary and Faversham Creek and supports a wide range of wildfowl, waders and raptors.

### Birds
Year round: Little Egret, wildfowl, waders, Marsh Harrier, Bearded Tit
Spring: Garganey, Little Stint, Curlew Sandpiper, Spotted Redshank, Ruff
Summer: Hobby, Avocet, Little Tern, Reed and Sedge Warblers
Autumn: Garganey, Osprey, passage waders (including Little Stint, Curlew Sandpiper), Little Gull, Black Tern
Winter: Red-breasted Merganser, Merlin, Hen Harrier, Stonechat, Twite.

## Management
Managed by the Kent Wildlife Trust.

## Opening times and access
There is open access at all times along waymarked paths. A visitor centre is open weekends and bank holidays 11.00 until 17.00 (or dusk if earlier). There is disabled access to the visitor centre and two hides in the eastern half of the reserve. The southern car park is for use by the disabled only.

## Other amenities
All amenities can be found in nearby Oare village and Faversham.

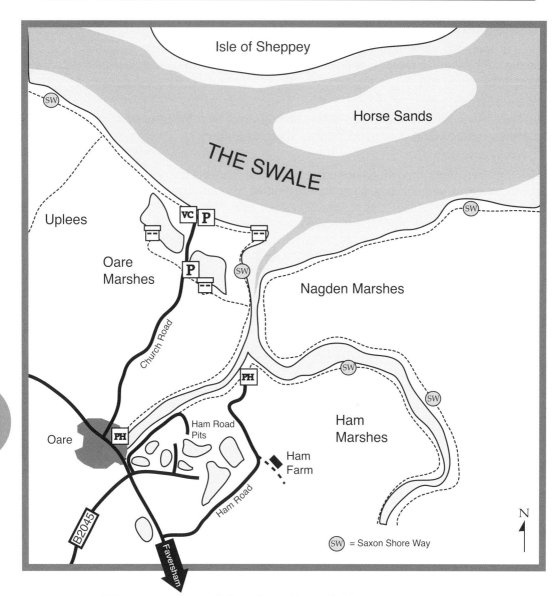

## Site 3.06 Oare Marshes Local Nature Reserve

### Location (car park TR013647 )

From the A2 west of Faversham take the B2045 north to Oare villag. Turn west then north onto Church Road (signposted "Harty Ferry"), which leads to the reserve.

### Birdwatching tips

This is arguably one of the best sites in the county for obtaining close views of waders. At high tide there are large numbers on the two main floods. Autumn wader passage from mid July to early October brings an excellent variety and impressive numbers of waders. Winds from the south-west in August and September sometimes result in substantial arrivals of passage waders, such as Greenshank and Curlew Sandpiper. There is a good spring wader passage in April and May. Seabirds such as skuas and more occasionally Leach's Petrel are sometimes seen during northerly winds. Rarities have included Cattle Egret, Little Bittern, Baillon's Crake, European Bee-eater, White-rumped Sandpiper, Long-billed Dowitcher, White-winged Black and Caspian Terns. Neaby Ham Road Pit is worth checking for diving duck

## 3.07 South Swale Local Nature Reserve and Seasalter

A Kent Wildlife Trust reserve comprising coastal farmland, reed-filled ditches and open shore including saltmarsh, shingle beach and mudflats.

### Birds

Year round: Marsh Harrier, waders, Bearded Tit
Summer: Little Tern, Reed and Sedge Warblers
Autumn: Gannet, skuas, Little Gull, terns, Whinchat, Wheatear
Winter: Red-throated Diver, Dark-bellied Brent Goose, Wigeon, Golden Plover, Hen Harrier, Merlin, Short-eared Owl, Snow and Lapland Buntings.

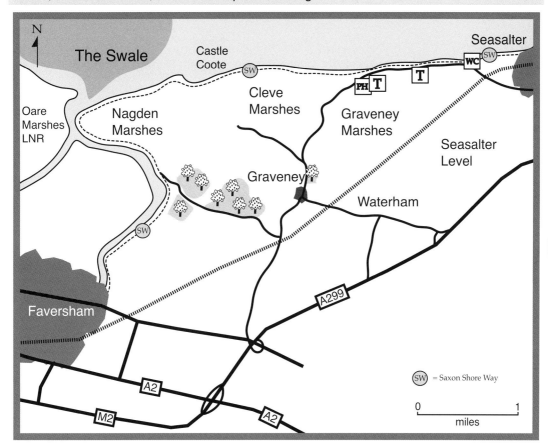

53

## Site 3.07 South Swale Local Nature Reserve and Seasalter

### Location (car park TR061646)

Situated on the south side of the Swale estuary north of Graveney Marshes and alongside Faversham Creek. Take the minor road north from the M2/A2/A299 junction towards Graveney. Continue through Graveney for 1 mile and park sensibly by the road near Ye Olde Sportsman public house.

### Management

Managed by the Kent Wildlife Trust.

### Opening times and access

There is open access at all times along public footpaths.

### Other amenities

Ye Olde Sportsman public house serves food and drink. Public toilets are at Seasalter. All other amenities can be found in Whitstable and Faversham.

## Birdwatching tips

Check the reedy ditches for Bearded Tit. A rising tide brings shorebirds closer to the footpath. Please avoid the shingle beach at Castle Coote, since this is a sensitive area for breeding terns and roosting waders. Northerly or easterly winds may produce seabirds in autumn. Divers, grebes and seaduck are usually present between Seasalter and Whitstable in winter. Recent rarities have included White-tailed Eagle, Sociable Plover, Desert and Paddyfield Warblers and Blyth's Pipit.

## 3.08 Conyer Creek

An area of coastal farmland and scrub with reed-filled ditches and views over the Swale Estuary.

### Birds

Year round: Little Egret, Marsh Harrier, Water Rail, waders, Kingfisher, Bearded Tit, Corn Bunting
Summer: Little Tern, Cuckoo, warblers
Autumn: Osprey, passage waders, Whinchat, Wheatear
Winter: Grebes, Dark-bellied Brent Goose, Red-breasted Merganser, waders, Fieldfare, Redwing.

54

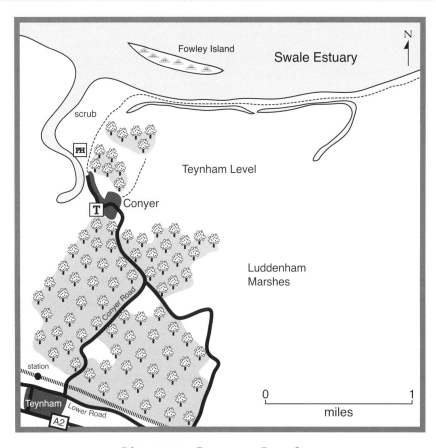

### Site 3.08 Conyer Creek

## Location (TQ959651)

From the A2 in Teynham take Station Road north. Turn right onto Lower Road and then turn north onto Conyer Road to reach Conyer village after 1.25 miles. There is limited roadside parking near the Ship Inn.

### Opening times and access
There is open access at all times along public footpaths.

### Other amenities
The Ship Inn serves food and drink. All other amenities can be found in Teynham.

### Birdwatching tips
Check the reedy ditches for Bearded Tit and Water Rail, although the latter is more likely to be heard than seen. Red-breasted Mergansers often congregate around Fowley Island, where Avocets roost. Osprey has become a regular visitor in recent autumns.

## 3.09 Murston
A variety of habitats comprising lakes, reedbeds, woodland and scrub adjacent to the Swale Estuary. The area attracts a wide variety of species throughout the year but is at its best during winter and passage periods.

### Birds
Year round: Kingfisher, Bearded Tit, Corn Bunting
Summer: Little Tern, warblers
Autumn: passage waders (including Greenshank, Whimbrel, Curlew Sandpiper)
Winter: Red-throated Diver, grebes, Bittern, Dark-bellied Brent Goose, Goldeneye, Scaup, Red-breasted Merganser, Fieldfare, Redwing.

### Opening times and access
There is open access at all times along public footpaths. Please keep to footpaths and avoid the fishing lakes, which are privately owned and access is discouraged. Bus services serve the Murston area of Sittingbourne. There is a cycle route running through the area.

### Other amenities
All amenities can be found in Sittingbourne.

### Birdwatching tips
The pits adjacent to the seawall are a regular haunt of scarce grebes in hard weather, Red-breasted Merganser and diving duck (including Scaup) in winter. The Swale holds a wide variety of waders that are best viewed two-three hours either side of high tide. This is a regular site for Bittern during the winter, although the birds are typically elusive. Rarities have included Black Stork, Red-breasted Goose, Black Brant and Common Yellowthroat.

### Warning
Car thieves and other undesirables sometimes frequent the area so please take care and do not leave valuables in your vehicle.

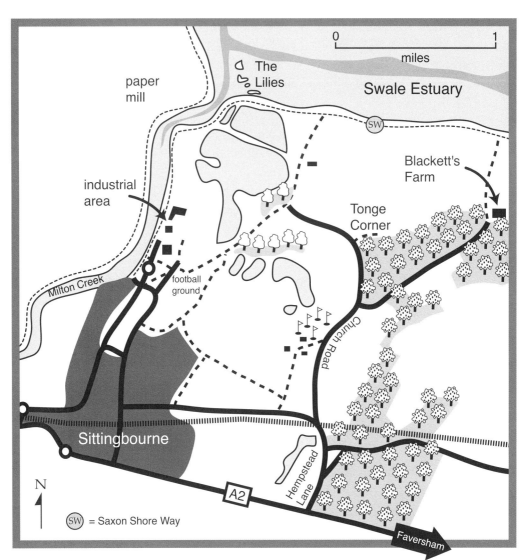

**Site 3.09 Murston**

## Location (TQ927655)
Situated on the south side of the Swale Estuary north of Sittingbourne. Parking is difficult at this site and it is perhaps best to park on the roadside in the Industrial Estate near Milton Creek.

# CHAPTER 4 Thames and Medway Estuaries

## Introduction

These two major estuaries combine with the Swale Estuary to form one of the most important intertidal areas in the whole of the UK. Supporting internationally important numbers of wildfowl and waders during the winter and migration periods, these wild areas are surrounded on the southern and western edges by the built up areas of the Medway towns and Gravesend. Much of the Hoo Peninsula is dominated by reclaimed fresh marshes with an increasing area being managed by the RSPB. The area is of exceptional wildlife interest with the RSPB managing land at Cliffe Pools and around Northward Hill. The Medway Estuary comprises a wonderful maze of tidal creeks, islands and saltmarsh. Much of this is difficult to access, but the southern shore in particular offers some superb opportunities to watch birds. The downs to the south provide a scenic backdrop to the area with some locations still holding a good variety of woodland species including Hawfinch.

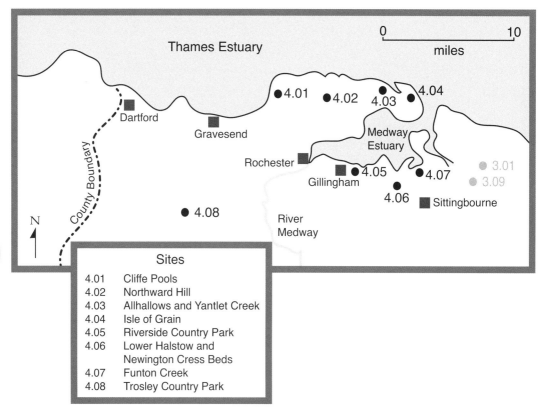

**Map: Thames and Medway Estuaries**

## Special birds

The area is internationally important for its concentrations of wintering wildfowl and waders, supporting similar species to those found in the Swale or on Sheppey. All of Kent's regular wintering species of ducks and waders are present in considerable numbers. The pools at Cliffe host large numbers of diving duck including Goldeneyes and in most winters scarcer species such as Scaup, Long-tailed Duck and Smew. The scarcer grebes are often to be found in the sheltered creeks of the Medway Estuary or the pools at Cliffe during the winter. Breeding waders include Avocet, Lapwing and Redshank. Passage waders such as Spotted

Redshank, Greenshank, Ruff, Common and Green Sandpipers all occur in good numbers during spring and autumn, whilst this area regularly hosts Wood Sandpiper, Curlew Sandpiper and Little Stint with rare waders appearing annually. Although not quite as good for raptors as Sheppey, the Hoo Peninsula in particular supports wintering Hen Harrier and Merlin with Marsh Harrier and Peregrine recorded throughout the year. Common Buzzard regularly winters at Northward Hill, whilst Hobby is an increasingly common summer visitor. Scarce species such as Osprey and Montagu's Harrier are regular visitors. The area supports significant populations of wintering Short-eared Owl, with Barn and Little Owls also well represented. Yellow-legged Gull can be found in good numbers at Higham, especially during the late summer and early autumn. There is a regular passage of skuas and other seabirds during the autumn.

## Timing

Birdwatching in this area is excellent throughout the year. The first evidence of the arrival of spring is the return of Grey Herons to the heronry at Northward Hill in late January. The first spring migrants are usually in evidence by late March with Wheatear, Sand Martin and possibly Garganey likely to be present. During April, Avocet, Redshank, Lapwing and Oystercatcher start breeding whilst Ruff and Common Sandpiper are amongst the wide variety of passage waders moving through the area. During May less common migrants such as Curlew Sandpiper, Little Stint and Wood Sandpiper may appear and there is always a good chance of finding a rare migrant.

During the summer the large colonies of gulls, and to a lesser extent, Common, Sandwich and Little Terns, are a feature of the Medway. A Little Egret colony has become established at Northward Hill in recent years.

Signs of autumn migration are noticeable as early as late June when the first Ruff and Green Sandpiper appear. By mid July autumn wader migration is in full swing, with a selection of passage waders in evidence. Numbers and variety remain relatively high throughout August and the first half of September. In recent years, July has seen the build up of large numbers of Little Egret at Northward Hill with several hundred recorded during July-September. This period is also notable for a peak in numbers of Yellow-legged Gull. September and October are excellent periods for searching out interesting passerine migrants at Grain with the chance of something more unusual such as a Red-backed Shrike or Yellow-browed Warbler.

Seabird passage commences in late August and continues well into December during periods of northerly/easterly winds. All four skuas are regularly seen and movements of Gannet, terns, Kittiwake, divers and auks can, at times, be spectacular. Scarcer species such as Sabine's Gull, Leach's Petrel, Little Auk and Sooty Shearwater are also noted from time to time.

By December huge concentrations of wintering wildfowl and waders are present in the area. Grebes and diving ducks are prominent at Cliffe and in the Medway Estuary whilst gull watchers will find much to occupy their time. Flocks of Corn Buntings and finches can be found at several locations and there is an impressive corvid roost at Northward Hill.

## 4.01 Cliffe Pools

An RSPB reserve comprising saline lagoons, freshwater pools, grassland, saltmarsh and scrub.

### Birds

Year round: Great Crested and Little Grebes, Little Egret, wildfowl, waders, Barn Owl, Stonechat
Spring: Spoonbill, Garganey, Black-tailed Godwit, Spotted Redshank, Ruff
Summer: Spoonbill, Hobby, Avocet, Turtle Dove, Nightingale, warblers
Autumn: Curlew Sandpiper, Little Stint, Spotted Redshank, Ruff
Winter: ducks, waders, Hen Harrier, Merlin, Peregrine, Short-eared Owl, Fieldfare, Redwing.

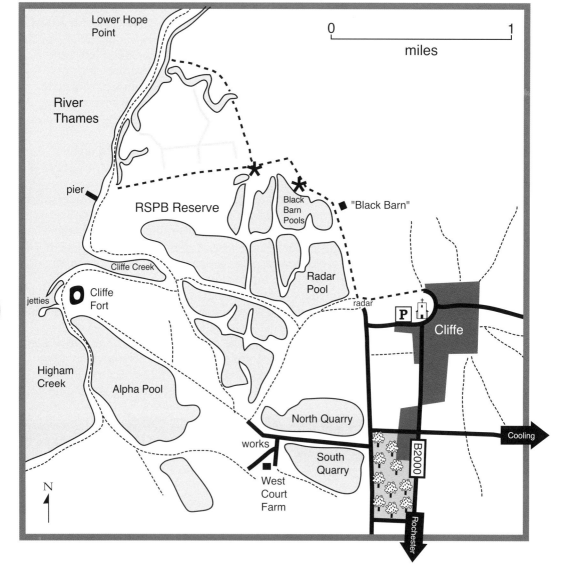

## Site 4.01 Cliffe Pools

### Location (car park TQ734765)

Take the A289 off the A2 near Strood. From the A289 follow the B2000 into the village of Cliffe. There is a bus service to Cliffe which stops at the Six Bells Pub.

## Management
Managed by the RSPB.

## Opening times and access
There is open access at all times along public footpaths.

## Other amenities
Amenities, including public toilets and a public house may be found in nearby Cliffe.

## Birdwatching tips
Viewing mounds afford excellent views across the reserve. High tide is most productive for roosting waders. This site is perhaps at its best during the autumn wader migration when large flocks of waders are usually present and a wide variety of species is likely to be encountered. Rare and scarce species are regular with Spoonbill, Temminck's Stint, Pectoral Sandpiper and Red-necked Phalarope all recorded in most years. Rarer species have included American Wigeon, Canvasback, White-rumped, Buff-breasted, Stilt and Marsh Sandpipers, several Broad-billed Sandpipers, Lesser Yellowlegs, Pallid Swift, Short-toed Lark and Aquatic Warbler. Periods of cold weather are likely to bring scarcer grebes, divers, Scaup, Long-tailed Duck and perhaps the occasional Glaucous or Iceland Gull.

Note that this site is being rapidly developed by the RSPB and visiting arrangements will change. Check the RSPB website or telephone the reserve office for current details (01634 222480).

## Non-bird interest
A range of wildlife includes Water Vole, Harvest Mouse and notable insects such as Scarce Emerald Damselfly, Shrill Carder bee and Green Hairstreak butterfly.

## Warning
The site has had a history of abuse from fly-tipping, unauthorised trail biking and other similar activities, but recent work undertaken by the RSPB has now greatly reduced these activities so that the reserve is largely safe for visitors. Please note that some of the lagoons are very deep.

## 4.02 Northward Hill

This RSPB reserve features a mixture of woodland and wet grassland. It supports a good population of Nightingales and the wood has the largest heronry in the UK, with around 150 pairs of Grey Herons and 40 pairs of Little Egrets nesting. The RSPB has recently expanded the reserve by purchasing areas of flooded grassland, reedbed and scrub.

### Birds

Year round: Grey Heron, Little Egret, Marsh Harrier, Barn and Long-eared Owls, Corn Bunting
Spring and summer: Garganey, Avocet, Lapwing, Redshank, Yellow Wagtail
Autumn: passage waders (including Ruff, Common, Green and Wood Sandpipers), Whinchat, Wheatear
Winter: Hen Harrier, Common Buzzard, Merlin, Peregrine, Lapwing, Golden Plover, Short-eared Owl, Fieldfare, Redwing, corvids, Tree Sparrow.

### Management

Managed by the RSPB.

### Opening times and access

Public paths open at all times. The gates at Eastborough Bungalow are locked at dusk. There are three nature trails, the shortest 600 yards, the longest 2.5 miles. The public footpath to the marshes is a 4 mile round trip. A "Heron Trail" from High Halstow village (signed from the Red Dog public house) runs around the wood, taking in a heronry viewing area and joining trails linking the viewpoints. Visits to other parts of the reserve are by prior arrangement only. There are steps and steep slopes that can become muddy in winter making access for the disabled difficult.

### Other amenities

All amenities can be found in High Halstow village.

### Birdwatching tips

The marshland viewpoints afford superb views across the low-lying fresh marshes. There is a large build up of Little Egrets between July and early September. An evening visit in winter is recommended to observe the spectacular concentrations of crows, pigeons and starlings flighting to roost. The area is excellent for birds of prey in winter and is a regular location for Common Buzzard. A walk across the farmland to Egypt and St Mary's Bays should produce a wide variety of shorebirds on the Thames. May is the best time to look for Nightingale. Rarities noted at this site have included Red-breasted Goose, Green-winged Teal, Crane, Black-winged Stilt and Marsh Sandpiper.

### Non-bird interest

Small Red-eyed Damselfly has been found in the fleets and ditches of this reserve. White-letter Hairstreak butterfly may be found here.

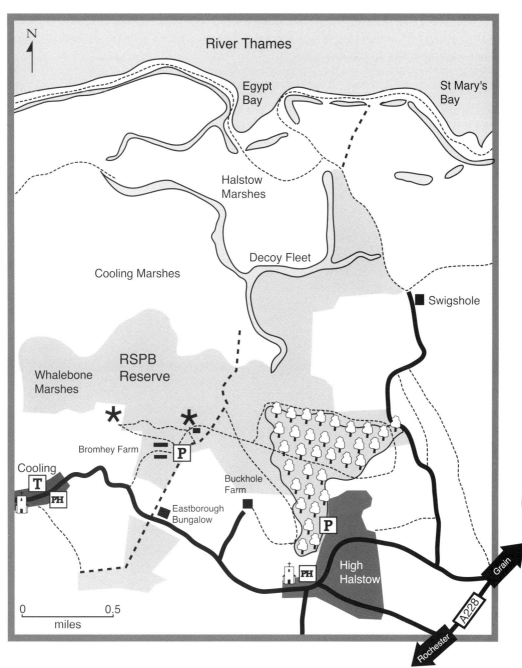

63

# Site 4.02 Northward Hill

**Location (car parks TQ781757 and TQ767763)**

Turn off the A228 Rochester to Grain road towards High Halstow. Once in High Halstow, take Harrison Drive and turn into Northwood Avenue to reach the car park at TQ781757. Alternatively, drive west from High Halstow towards Cooling and turn right at Eastborough bungalow (signed RSPB reserve) and follow to the car park at Bromhey Farm at TQ767763. An alternative car park for access to the Heronry viewpoint for the disabled is available by prior arrangement. Buses run from the Strood stop in High Halstow.

## 4.03 Allhallows and Yantlet Creek

An area of coastal farmland dominated by grassland and some arable farmland. Extensive mudflats are attractive to feeding waders.

### Birds

Year round: Little Egret, wildfowl, Marsh Harrier, waders, Corn Bunting
Spring and summer: Garganey, Lapwing, Redshank, Yellow Wagtail
Autumn: Gannet, passage waders, skuas, Kittiwake, terns
Winter: Red-throated Diver, Great Crested Grebe, Golden Plover, Lapland and Snow Buntings.

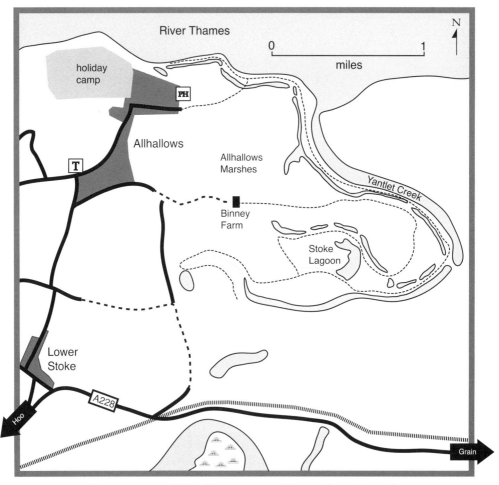

**Site 4.03 Allhallows and Yantlet Creek**

### Location (park at TQ844783)

From Rochester take the A228 towards Grain. At Lower Stoke take the minor road north to Allhallows. In Allhallows follow Avery Way to reach the British Pilot pub. There is on street parking here. A bus service from Strood stops outside the British Pilot.

### Opening times and access

There is open access at all times along public footpaths.

### Other amenities

Most amenities can be found in Allhallows village.

64

## Birdwatching tips

This has been a regular winter haunt of Lapland and Snow Buntings although numbers of the former have been low in recent winters. If present, Snow Buntings will usually be found on the small beaches or along the sea wall in the mouth of Yantlet Creek. It is worthwhile seawatching during the autumn when periods of northerly or easterly winds may produce movements of Gannet, skuas and sometimes Leach's Petrel or the occasional shearwater. A visit one or two hours either side of high tide will produce the best views of waders which are very distant when the tide is low. Visible migration can be interesting during light westerly winds when hirundines, wagtails, pipits and finches pass west into the Thames. Recent rarities have included Blue-winged Teal, Greater Yellowlegs and Gull-billed Tern.

## 4.04 Isle of Grain

Areas of coastal scrub, flooded clay pits and fleets situated at the mouth of the Thames and Medway Estuaries combine to produce an area which although low in aesthetic value is attractive to a wide variety of migrant species.

### Birds

Year round: wildfowl, waders
Autumn: Gannet, passage waders, skuas, Little Gull, Black Tern, auks, chats, warblers, flycatchers
Winter: Red-throated Diver, Great Crested Grebe, Snow Bunting.

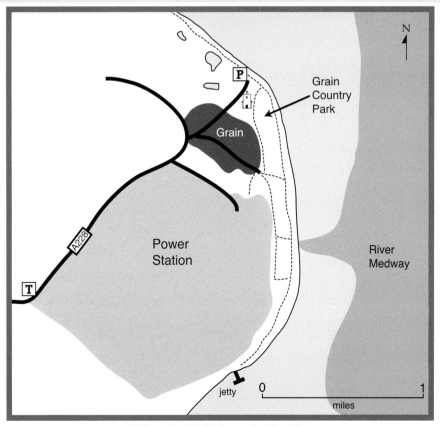

**Site 4.04 Isle of Grain**

65

## Location (car park TQ889770)

From Rochester take the A228 following signs to Grain. In Grain village turn left onto High Street and follow the road to the beach car park. A bus service from Strood serves Grain.

## Opening times and access

There is open access at all times along public footpaths.

## Other amenities

All amenities can be found in Grain village.

## Birdwatching tips

This site is worth a visit during the autumn and winter months. Winds from a northerly or easterly quarter will produce movements of seabirds sometimes including all four species of skua. Passerine migrants are most likely to be found during periods of easterly winds when Pied Flycatcher, Redstart and Whinchat can all be expected. This area has produced a number of rarer species including Bonelli's, Booted, Dusky, Icterine, Pallas's and Yellow-browed Warblers and Red-backed Shrike. Visible migration can be interesting during light winds from a westerly quarter when hirundines, wagtails, pipits and finches pass west into the Thames.

## Warning

Please keep to public rights of way and under no circumstances attempt to enter the fenced off areas of Grain Power Station.

## 4.05 Riverside Country Park

An area of scrub and coastal farmland with reedbeds adjacent to the Medway Estuary that supports large numbers of wintering wildfowl and waders.

### Birds

Year round: Little Egret, Oystercatcher, Redshank, gulls (including Mediterranean Gull)
Spring: Black-tailed Godwit
Summer: Black-headed Gull, Common Tern, Nightingale, Turtle Dove, Sedge, Reed and occasional Grasshopper Warblers
Autumn: Black-tailed Godwit, Spotted Redshank, occasional Black Tern
Winter: Black-necked and Slavonian Grebes, Dark-bellied Brent Goose, ducks (including Goldeneye and Red-breasted Merganser), waders.

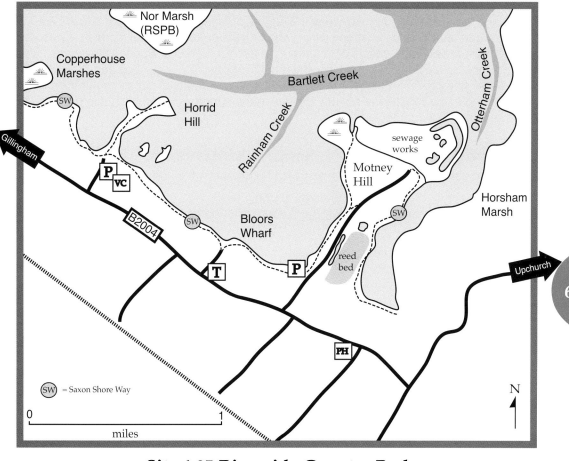

## Site 4.05 Riverside Country Park

### Location (car park TQ805684)

The main visitor centre car park may be accessed from the B2004 1 mile north of Gillingham. From the car park it is possible to walk the 1 mile round trip to Horrid Hill and view Nor Marsh (wheelchair and pushchair accessible), or the 3 mile round trip to Motney Hill (pushchair accessible). A bus service from Gillingham stops near the visitor centre (although not on Sundays in winter). Gillingham has good rail connections.

### Opening times and access

The visitor centre is open between 10:00 and 16:30. The main visitor centre car park is open 08:30 until dusk and closed Christmas and Boxing Days. The alternative car park at Motney Hill is always open. Otherwise, there is open access along public footpaths at all times. Cruises on the River Medway can be booked at the visitor centre (01634 378987).

### Other amenities

The visitor centre has a tea-room, displays and toilets. Other amenities are available in nearby Gillingham and Rainham.

### Management

Mainly operated as a country park by Medway Council, but the saltings of Nor Marsh and Motney Hill are RSPB reserves.

### Birdwatching tips

Best during the autumn and winter when the largest numbers of wildfowl and waders are present. Good after periods of strong winds when divers or seaduck may appear. A visit is perhaps most rewarding a couple of hours before or after high tide. Spotted Redshank regularly roost at Motney Hill during the autumn. One or two Black-necked and Slavonian Grebes are often present during the winter months. The occasional Grasshopper Warbler may be found in the reedbed at Motney Hill during the spring and summer. Little Egret is now present throughout the year.

## 4.06 Lower Halstow and Newington Cress Beds

An area of cress beds with woodland, scrub and orchards in the surrounding area.

### Birds

Winter: Water Rail, Jack Snipe, Green Sandpiper, Grey Wagtail, Chiffchaff.

### Opening times and access

There is public access at all times, but please ensure you keep to public rights of way.

### Other amenities

These are available in Lower Halstow and Newington.

### Birdwatching tips

The cress beds at Newington are worth a look in winter for Water Rail, Green Sandpiper and sometimes Jack Snipe. The scrub at Lower Halstow is a regular wintering site for Chiffchaff.

Medway

scrub

Funton Creek (4.07)

N

Upchurch

PH

Lower
Halstow

Hawes
Wood

Bog
Farm

P

industrial park

Rainham

station

PH

Newington

A2

Sittingbourne

69

0
1

miles

## Site 4.06 Lower Halstow and Newington Cress Beds

**Location (cress beds TQ862654)**

From the A2 in Newington, take the minor road north for 500 yards. At the staggered crossroads, turn north. There is a small pull-off by an industrial park. If this is occupied, park sensibly elsewhere and walk back to the site. Access is along the public footpath just south of the industrial park. A bus service serves Newington from both Sittingbourne and Gillingham. There is a railway station in Newington. For Lower Halstow, park on the housing estate north of the road through the village, close to the church.

## 4.07 Funton Creek

Of the many tidal creeks and saltmarsh islands that make up the Medway Estuary, this is perhaps the most easily accessible and offers some excellent birding throughout the year.

### Birds

Spring and autumn: Little Egret, Garganey, migrant waders including Greenshank, Black-tailed Godwit, Little Stint, Curlew Sandpiper, Wood and Common Sandpipers
Winter: wildfowl and waders, Hen and Marsh Harriers, Merlin, Peregrine.

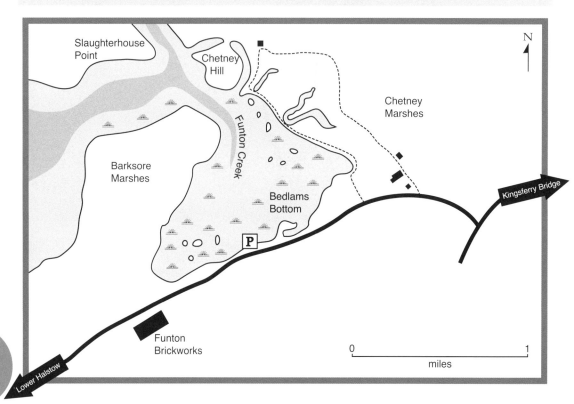

## Site 4.07 Funton Creek

### Location (roadside parking at TQ887684)

Take the minor road along the south shore of the Medway Estuary from Lower Halstow towards the Isle of Sheppey. There are several places you can pull off the road to view the estuary. Note that this road is liable to flooding and may be impassable during certain tides.

### Opening times and access

There is public access at all times. This site is especially suitable for those with mobility problems since many species can be observed from your car. Do not leave public footpaths in this sensitive area and under no circumstances attempt to access Barksore Marshes.

### Other amenities

These are available in nearby Iwade or Lower Halstow.

### Birdwatching tips

Best on a rising or falling tide. Several hundred Avocet and increasing numbers of Little Egret tend to roost on the saltmarsh at the adjacent Barksore Marshes. Small numbers of passage waders frequent the fleets on Chetney whilst small numbers of Bewick's Swans are often to be found on Chetney during the winter.

## 4.08 Trosley Country Park

An area of traditionally managed woodland on the North Downs that supports a good selection of commoner woodland species and is a regular site for Hawfinch.

### Birds

Year round: woodland birds, Marsh Tit, Hawfinch.

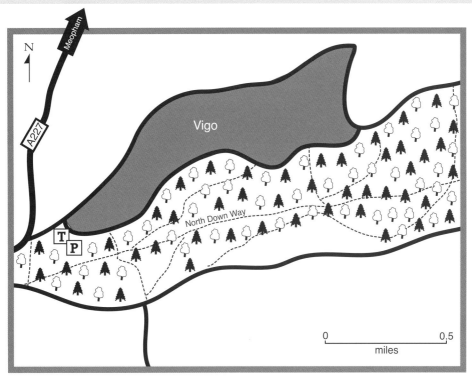

### Site 4.08 Trosley Country Park

### Location (car park TQ632610)

From junction 2 of the M20, travel north towards Meopham on the A227. Turn right into Vigo village and then right again. The entrance to the country park is in front of you on the gentle left hand bend. Please pay attention to the car park closing times that are displayed at the entrance.

### Management

Managed by Kent County Council.

### Opening times and access

The car park is open between 08:30 and 17:00, but public footpaths allow access at all times.

### Other amenities

There is a small visitor centre, information board and toilets. All other amenities are available in the nearby villages of Wrotham and Meopham.

### Birdwatching tips

An early start is advisable since the area is popular with dog walkers. Hawfinch is regularly found near the car park, late winter and spring being the best times to connect with this elusive species. Marsh Tit can usually be found near the car park too.

## CHAPTER 5 | Canterbury: The Blean and Stour Valley

### Introduction

On two sides of Canterbury are areas of impressive habitat. To the north is the great ancient wood known as The Blean, one of the largest blocks of semi-natural woodland left in England. Managed commercially for many years with planted sweet chestnut and conifers, much of the woodland is now managed by conservation organisations as a National Nature Reserve that includes the RSPB reserve at Church Wood. The sheer size of the wood makes the area impressive and worth a visit. To the north-east of the city, coal mining subsidence has allowed a substantial wetland of reedbeds, wet meadows, lakes and wet woodlands to develop along the valley of the Stour River. Further similar habitat has been inadvertently created by the gravel industry throughout the Stour River Valley, and more recently, English Nature has deliberately created more areas of wet meadows and reedbeds from arable land, and provided facilities to observe them making much of this area easily accessible. South of the city, on the chalk soils of the North Downs, there are areas of very different woodland, which provide additional variety.

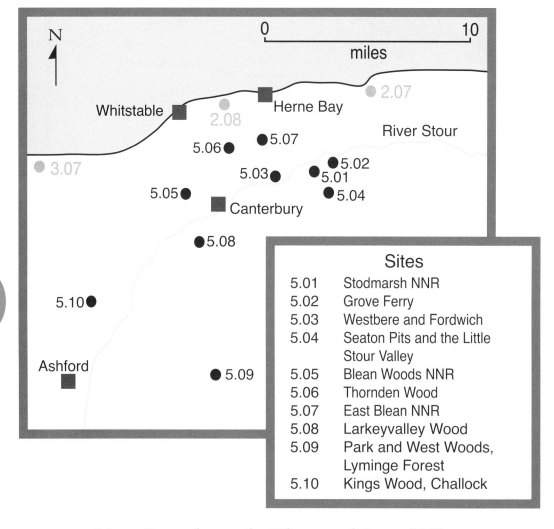

| Sites | |
|---|---|
| 5.01 | Stodmarsh NNR |
| 5.02 | Grove Ferry |
| 5.03 | Westbere and Fordwich |
| 5.04 | Seaton Pits and the Little Stour Valley |
| 5.05 | Blean Woods NNR |
| 5.06 | Thornden Wood |
| 5.07 | East Blean NNR |
| 5.08 | Larkeyvalley Wood |
| 5.09 | Park and West Woods, Lyminge Forest |
| 5.10 | Kings Wood, Challock |

**Map: Canterbury, the Blean and Stour Valley**

## Special birds

The large areas of woodland in The Blean are on some of the poorer soils in the area, the richer more fertile areas having been cleared for agriculture. However, there are fewer birds in these woodlands than you might expect, but the sheer scale of the woods is impressive and the site is well worth a visit. All three species of woodpeckers and Woodcock are present throughout the year and small numbers of Nightingales and Nightjars join them in the summer. Some woodland species such as Hawfinch and Willow Tit are declining in the county and their disappearance was first noted in these woods. Only very small numbers are now present, if at all, but the reasons for this decline are, as yet, unknown. Other species such as Turtle Dove and Spotted Flycatcher now arrive in spring in much smaller numbers and are increasingly hard to find. Some species, which were only ever present in very small numbers, like Wood Warbler, Redstart and Golden Oriole no longer breed although they still occur on spring migration. But there are still Marsh Tits and Lesser Spotted Woodpeckers, and birds of prey are increasing with Hobby, Common Buzzard and even Osprey using the woodlands. Kent birders expect them to be joined one day by Honey Buzzard and Red Kite and all these species are being seen more frequently, both here and in the woods on the Downs. In winter, all the woods are used by roosts of birds from the surrounding farmland, such as Redwing, Fieldfare and Brambling. Flocks of Common Crossbill, Siskin and Lesser Redpoll are worth scrutinising as rarities such as Arctic Redpoll have been recorded. The downland woods tend to be better for Tree Pipit, Nightjar and Woodcock, and at Lyminge Forest there is the added star attraction of Firecrest in spring and summer. A visit to look for these little jewels in the tops of the tallest conifers is a must for the birdwatcher who enjoys a challenge!

The wetlands of the Stour Valley are a fantastic place to look for birds and are home to several rare breeding species. The valley is a migration flyway, and this area is often the first place in the UK where birds, which are just starting to colonise Britain, choose to nest. Examples include Savi's and Cetti's Warblers. Birders in the county constantly speculate on "what next?" A spring visit for the first Garganey, Little Ringed Plover and Yellow Wagtail of the year is an annual ritual for many. Large numbers of Hobbies gather in the valley in spring and summer and other raptors such as Red-footed Falcon occasionally join them. Water Rail, Bearded Tit and Marsh Harrier breed and Bittern joins them in winter. In recent years in spring and summer Purple Heron, Little Bittern, Black Kite, Baillon's Crake and Slender-billed Gull have all been seen. In winter, Peregrine, Merlin and Hen Harrier arrive along with many wildfowl. An evening visit to experience Hen and Marsh Harriers floating in to roost, whilst large numbers of Fieldfare and Redwing, Starling, crows and pigeons fill the sky is a great experience. The recent run of mild winters seems to have reduced the occurrence of wintering flocks of White-fronted Geese and Bewick's Swans and the once regular Great Grey Shrike now rarely occurs, but there are still plenty of other birds to be seen.

73

## Timing

The woodlands are best from late autumn through winter and into spring. The resident species, including trickier species such as Lesser Spotted Woodpecker, are most easily seen from mid February to early April when they are most vocal. At this time, migrating Siskin, Lesser Redpoll and Brambling pass through. From mid April onwards, Willow Warbler, Chiffchaff, Blackcap, Garden Warbler, Nightingale and Tree Pipit are present. This is the time of year to search for Firecrest. These species are most vocal early in the morning but there is an evening chorus too. As most species go quiet as night falls, the song of the Nightingale becomes more powerful and evocative. An evening visit at this time should allow you to hear and perhaps see Tawny Owl and Woodcock. The latter perform their roding display flight at dusk, when they fly in wide circles over the woodland making strange grunting and whistling noises. A month later and Nightingales have almost stopped singing but the strange, mechanical churring of Nightjars fills the night sky. Things are quieter from June through to late September, when the woods begin to fill again with winter visitors and the resident species begin to flock together, calling constantly to keep together and becoming more visible as the canopy thins.

The wetlands in the Stour Valley sites are always worth visiting. Migration never stops. In mid March, before the true summer migrants begin to arrive, Yellow Wagtail, Garganey, Sand Martin and Water Pipit move through. By May, the wetland warblers; Cetti's, Reed, Sedge and sometimes Grasshopper and Savi's, join Lesser Whitethroat, Whitethroat and Nightingale in the scrub in a rich chorus. By the time the last spring migrants arrive in mid June, the first returning Green Sandpiper is back, leading the way for a continuous stream of waders moving through the valley from late summer; Ruff, Wood Sandpiper, Black-tailed Godwit and many others. Rarities are migrants too, and Purple Heron, Honey Buzzard, Spoonbill and Osprey are regularly seen in spring. Large flocks of Hobbies gather in the valley in late spring and summer and by late summer the flocks of moulting Garganeys are joined by the first returning Shoveler, Pochard and Teal, which build up in numbers through the winter. August is a good time to look for Spotted Crake, which has been regular at Grove Ferry in recent years. Waders pour through in September and Water Pipit, Chiffchaff and Stonechat join the resident Cetti's Warblers through the winter months. The sky is constantly full of parties of finches, Fieldfare, Redwing, pigeons and crows but the star birds are the raptors; Hen and Marsh Harriers roost in the reedbed, where Bittern, Water Rail and Bearded Tit remain throughout the year but are more easily seen at this time. Any waterbody holds flocks of ducks and few have a reputation as good as Seaton Pits for the variety of diving ducks that can be seen. Search among the Tufted Ducks and Pochards for Smew, Scaup or other rarer species.

## 5.01 Stodmarsh National Nature Reserve

This is the most accessible of the three sites in the Stour Valley (see also 5.02 and 5.03). It is a beautiful place giving a sense of wildness and the feeling of a true river valley with an excellent mix of habitats including river, reedbed, open water, grazing marsh, scrub and wet woodland.

### Birds

Year round: Marsh Harrier, Cetti's Warbler, Bearded Tit, Water Rail
Spring: Garganey, Nightingale, Osprey, warblers, Hobby, Yellow Wagtail
Summer: Hobby, Spoonbill, Garganey, Savi's Warbler, Yellow Wagtail
Winter: Bittern, wildfowl, Hen Harrier, Water Pipit.

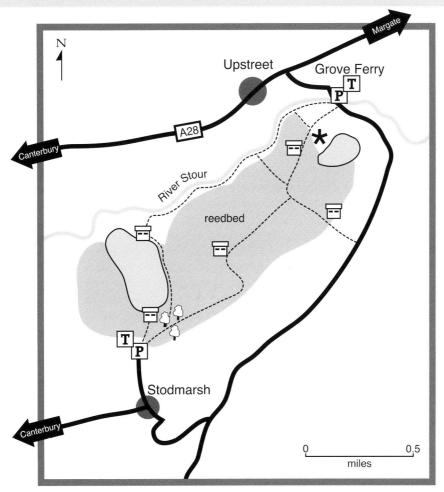

## Sites 5.01 and 5.02 Stodmarsh NNR and Grove Ferry

### Location (car park TR221609)

Stodmarsh is located 3 miles from the centre of Canterbury south of the A28. The reserve car park is located a few hundred yards from Stodmarsh village. It is signposted from the main street next to the Red Lion Pub (which is an excellent place to eat).

### Management

Stodmarsh is a National Nature Reserve managed by English Nature.

## Opening times and access

The car park and reserve are open at all times. The reserve trails are well signposted. One hide is fully accessible to all and there is an easy access trail to some of the best areas of wet woodland. Public footpaths including the long distance Stour Valley Walk cross the reserve. There are several circular walks through this area. The nearest railway station is Sturry (see 5.03). Dogs are allowed on the footpaths but not the nature trails. It is possible to walk from this site to Grove Ferry (Site 5.02).

## Other amenities

There is a toilet and notice board at the car park. An information leaflet and map is available. There are pubs in most of the villages and plenty of places to eat in Canterbury.

## Birdwatching tips

The areas of wet woodland close to the car park are accessible along the easy access trail and are good for small birds including Siskin and Lesser Redpoll during the winter. Cetti's Warbler can be heard in winter and spring around the car park and from almost any patch of scrub in the reedbeds. Scan the open water for wildfowl at any time of year from either of the hides or the raised footpath known as the Lampen Wall; good numbers are present throughout the year, especially in winter.

Stodmarsh is a place where you must scan the skies. In winter, especially at dawn and dusk, large flocks of Fieldfares and Redwings, corvids, Cormorants and gulls move up and down the valley. An evening visit in winter is especially rewarding; stand on the Lampen Wall as Marsh and Hen Harriers fly in to roost and you might see a Barn Owl or Merlin. In spring anything could fly over, and in summer look out for hirundines and Marsh Harrier. Check the flocks of Hobbies in May and June for Red-footed Falcon, an almost annual visitor. In winter, Water Pipit is best seen at the "tideline" along this section, especially where the reeds have been flattened. Throughout the year, wherever there is reed, Bearded Tit and Water Rail can be seen or heard. The best chance of seeing a Bittern is from the Reedbed hide during the winter or from the Lampen Wall in late February and March when up to 16 have been seen performing pre-migration "croaking" flights. Garganey and Water Pipit are often present in spring and Yellow Wagtail and Hobby in summer. Rarities have included Ferruginous Duck, American Coot, Marsh Sandpiper and Yellow-browed Warbler.

## Warning

The paths can be very muddy in winter and are sometimes closed. Heed all warning signs.

## 5.02 Grove Ferry

**76**

This wetland is part of Stodmarsh National Nature Reserve and was created by English Nature in 1995. It shares many features of Stodmarsh itself (Site 5.01) yet has a very different feel to it. It is well worth visiting both sites, which can easily be done in a day.

### Birds

Year round: Marsh Harrier, Cetti's Warbler, Bearded Tit, Water Rail
Spring: Garganey, Nightingale, Osprey
Summer: Hobby, Little Ringed Plover
Autumn: waders, Spotted Crake
Winter: wildfowl, Hen Harrier, Water Pipit, Ruff.

### Location (car park TR239630) See Site 5.01 for map

The car park is located next to the Grove Ferry public house at Grove Ferry, just south of the A28 some 4 miles east of Canterbury.

### Management

This is part of Stodmarsh National Nature Reserve, managed by English Nature.

## Opening times and access

The car park and reserve are open at all times. This site is not as accessible for the less abled as Stodmarsh (Site 5.01). Two long distance walks; the Saxon Shore Way and the Stour Valley Walk give access to the site along with other public and permissive footpaths. Circular walks are possible between here and Stodmarsh. There are bus services from Thanet and Canterbury. It is possible to walk from this site to Stodmarsh (Site 5.01).

## Other amenities

Toilets are open at the Grove Ferry car park between 09:00 and 16:30.

## Birdwatching tips

Cross the road from the car park and walk to the viewing mound. This offers open viewing over an area of shallow water which is excellent for birdwatching. There are wildfowl in the winter as well as Golden Plover, Lapwing and Ruff. In early spring look out for the first Sand Martin, Little Ringed Plover, Yellow Wagtail and Garganey here. Waders occur all year, and recently have included Temminck's Stint, Pectoral and Marsh Sandpipers. No sooner has spring migration stopped than autumn passage begins. This is also a good raised vantage point to scan the skies for raptors and other birds.

The two hides can allow good views of secretive reedbed birds such as Bittern and Water Rail. Listen out for the squeals and grunts of Water Rail and the "pinging" calls of Bearded Tit as you walk around the trail. Scan carefully anywhere the reed edge meets open water; in recent years in late summer and autumn Spotted Crake has frequently been seen here.

An early morning or dusk visit in spring is an especially wonderful experience with the reedbeds and scrub thick with the chatter of singing warblers (including Cetti's) and Nightingale. Garganey and Water Pipit are often present in spring and Yellow Wagtail and Hobby in summer. Rarities include Baillon's Crake, White-rumped and Sharp-tailed Sandpipers, Slender-billed Gull, Red-rumped Swallow and Aquatic Warbler.

## Warning

The paths can be wet and sticky in winter and are sometimes flooded and closed. Heed on-site warning signs.

## 5.03 Westbere and Fordwich

This area is less well watched than Sites 5.01 and 5.02 and is not specifically managed for conservation. It consequently has fewer birds. However, it has a different feel to it with greater amounts of woodland. There is no official car parking area but it is the most easily accessible site in the Stour Valley by rail. It shares many of the habitats and species with 5.01 and 5.02.

### Birds

Year round: Cetti's Warbler, Water Rail, Marsh Harrier
Spring and summer: Hobby, warblers
Winter: wildfowl, Hen Harrier, Bittern.

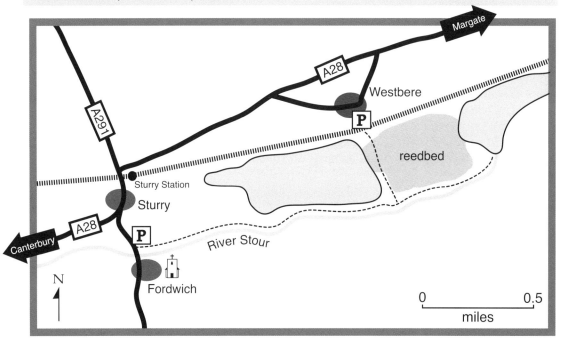

## Site 5.03 Westbere and Fordwich

### Location (car parks TR179598 and TR196610)

Just north-east of Canterbury south of the villages of Sturry and Westbere south of the A28. Access is via public rights of way from the minor road in Sturry at TR179598 or from the village of Westbere at TR196610.

### Opening times and access

This site is open and accessible at all times.

### Other amenities

All amenities in Canterbury.

### Birdwatching tips

From Sturry railway station, walk 600 yards towards Fordwich and turn left onto the public footpath just before the tiny road bridge. By car, park just off the Fordwich Road in a small road like Brooklands and take the footpath. Alternatively, park in Westbere close to Walnut Tree Lane. Cross the railway and take the path until it joins the main track along the River Stour. This path is well maintained and can be followed as far as you want, examining all areas of open water, woodland and scrub and reedbed. You will have to return to your point of access by the same route. It is not possible to walk to Stodmarsh (Site 5.01) from here as the river bank has been breached.

There is a lot of scrub and taller willow and alder trees along the walk, all worth examining for woodland species, which in winter regularly include Chiffchaff, Lesser Redpoll and Siskin. Cetti's Warbler is present throughout the year and other warblers arrive in spring. Bittern, Water Rail and Bearded Tit are all present although perhaps harder to see than at Sites 5.01 and 5.02. Marsh Harrier can be seen throughout the year, the large flock of Hobbies that often gathers in the valley can be watched from here and Hen Harriers float through in winter. The lakes are sometimes disturbed by fishermen, but a few wildfowl can usually be seen. Like the rest of this valley, watch out overhead as anything might fly over! Rarities include Ferruginous and Ring-necked Ducks, Great White Egret and Crane.

## Warning
The public footpath along the Stour Valley is regularly cut off by flooding west of Stodmarsh in winter. The section beyond the path to Westbere is through nettlebeds!

## 5.04 Seaton Pits and the Little Stour Valley
This small attractive site is just south of Stodmarsh in the valley of the Little Stour, east of the village of Wickhambreaux.

### Birds
Year round: Kingfisher, Grey Wagtail, woodpeckers, Sparrowhawk
Spring: warblers
Winter: wildfowl including Smew, harriers, Bittern, Firecrest.

## Opening times and access
Open at all times; access is only possible along the public footpath. This gives good views of the main lake to the north. There is no access to the other lakes or the woodland around the site.

## Other amenities
There are lots of good pubs in the area. The nearest toilets are at Stodmarsh (Site 5.01).

## Birdwatching tips
Walk the footpath scanning the gravel pits for waterbirds and the scrub for warblers in spring and summer. Keep your eye on the river to your right for Kingfisher and Grey Wagtail. Walk as far as you want and return by the same route. Alternatively, the public footpath crosses the Little Stour at Deadman's Bridge and runs alongside Wenderton Wood. From here it is possible to follow public and permissive footpaths onto Deerson and Preston Marshes which eventually lead around Preston village and back to Seaton. This circular walk is especially recommended in winter as the marshes can hold harriers, geese and wildfowl. Look out for Countryside Stewardship Scheme notices and map boards showing access routes on gate posts.

## Warning
The path is very wet in winter.

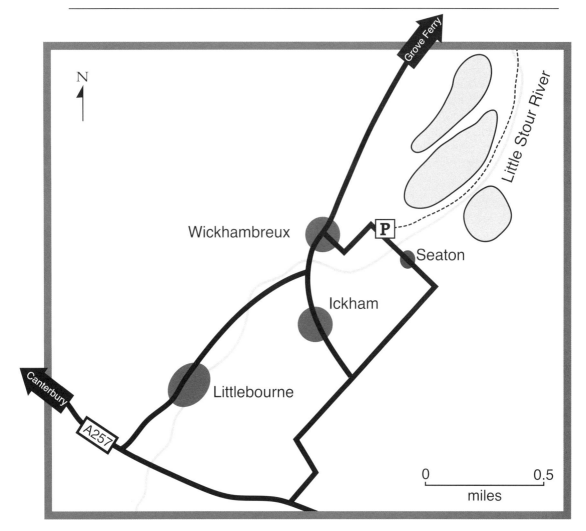

## Site 5.04 Seaton Pits and the Little Stour Valley

**Location (car park TR225588)**

Access is from the public footpath that leaves the minor road that runs from Wickhambreux to Seaton at TR225588. There is limited parking at this site, either by the small recreation ground or along the verge by the access stile.

## 5.05 Blean Woods National Nature Reserve

A National Nature Reserve with the best marked, most accessible trails and rights of way of the woods in this section. It contains open areas, coppiced woodland and mature forest.

### Birds

Year round: common woodland species including Lesser Spotted Woodpecker, Marsh Tit
Summer: Nightingale, Tree Pipit, Nightjar, Woodcock.

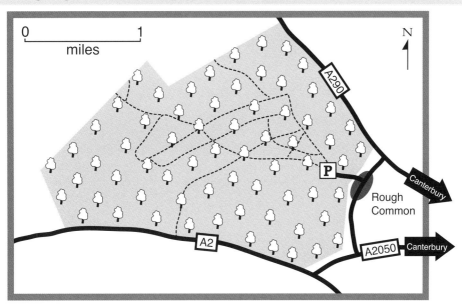

## Site 5.05 Blean Woods National Nature Reserve

### Location (car park TR123594)

The RSPB reserve car park is signposted from Rough Common village on the north-west side of Canterbury. Rough Common is along a minor road linking the A290 to Whitstable with the A2050 linking Canterbury to the A2.

### Management

Church Wood is a National Nature Reserve, owned by English Nature, the Woodland Trust and the RSPB, and managed by the RSPB.

### Opening times and access

The wood is accessible at all times. The car park is open from 08:00 to 21:00 daily. There is a height restriction on access to the car park. Entry is free. There is an information board and leaflets available in the car park. There are several well marked and maintained trails ranging in length from 1 to 8 miles. The green trail is suitable for wheelchairs. Canterbury East and Canterbury West railway stations are both 2 miles distant, and the Canterbury to Rough Common bus service stops at the reserve entrance.

### Other amenities

There is a post office, small store and a public house in Rough Common.

### Birdwatching tips
This is a large woodland on poor soils and birds can sometimes seem quite scarce. However, a trip in early spring should produce most of the resident species including Lesser Spotted Woodpecker and from mid April onwards there are Nightingales and a few Tree Pipits. Woodcock can be seen throughout the spring and early summer at dusk and from mid May a few pairs of Nightjar are present. The green route is the best trail for Nightingale. The area of woodland just after you cross the heath is a good place for Lesser Spotted Woodpecker. Nightjar and Tree Pipit can be found around the heathland.

### Non-bird interest
Heath Fritillary butterflies can be seen from mid June to mid July.

### Warning
The paths can be wet in winter but probably less so than other sites in this area.

## 5.06 Thornden Wood
This huge woodland contains mature oak forest as well as coppiced chestnut, conifers and several open areas. It is a large site with lots of paths and can be busy at times. Three open areas close to the car parks are excellent for Nightjars and Woodcock.

### Birds
Year round: common woodland species
Spring and summer: Tree Pipit, Nightjar, Woodcock, Nightingale, Turtle Dove, warblers
Winter: Lesser Redpoll, Siskin, Common Crossbill.

### Management
The wood has been a little run down in recent years with trails and marker posts in need of repair, but Thornden was purchased by Kent Wildlife Trust in 2003, so expect management to improve in the near future.

### Opening times and access
The wood is open at all times. There is a height restriction on access to the car parks.

### Other amenities
There are extensive permissive paths in addition to the public rights of way and rides. There are maps in the car parks.

### Birdwatching tips
Park in the northern car park. Take the middle route of the three that leave this car park and walk along the ride for several hundred yards until you come to an open area. This is a good place in spring for Tree Pipit, Nightjar and Woodcock. It also affords views across open sky for raptors and to surrounding tree tops. Either return directly to the car park, or turn right following the edge of the open area. Ignore the first path off to the right but take the next right to view a second large clearing for similar species to the first. Go round this, turning right, right, left and right to get back to the car park. This route takes you through both mature pine and deciduous stands.

An alternative route is to park at the southern car park, cross the road and walk several hundred yards along the straight ride. There is an open area on your right that is good for Tree Pipit, Nightjar and Woodcock. The wood is crossed by many paths, trails and rides. Other routes may be worth exploring.

### Warning
Do not leave valuables on view in your car. Take a torch and insect repellent if going out at dusk. The paths are uneven and are wet in winter and after heavy rain.

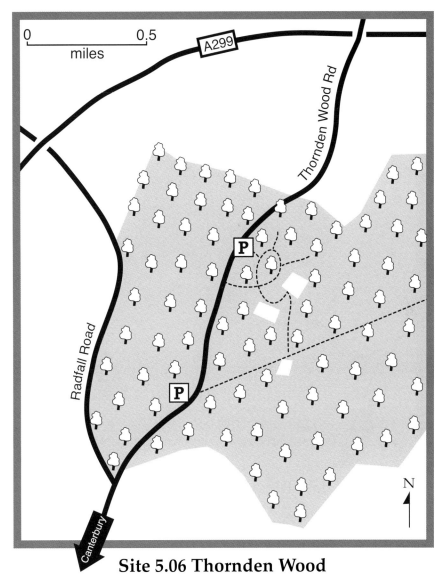

## Site 5.06 Thornden Wood

**Location (car parks TR147641 and TR143632)**

The two car parks are off Thornden Wood Road that runs north-south between Herne Bay and north Canterbury. Both car parks are well signposted.

## 5.07 East Blean National Nature Reserve

East Blean is a small wood containing a mixture of mature oak woodland with stands of ash, hornbeam and sweet chestnut coppice.

### Birds

Year round: common woodland species including Lesser Spotted Woodpecker
Summer: Nightingale.

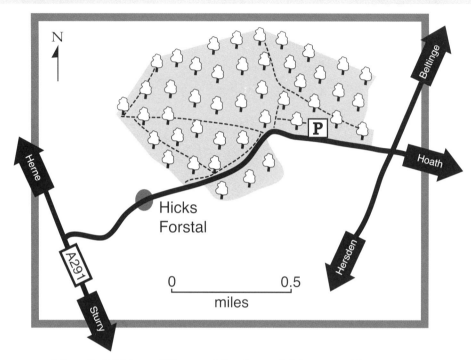

## Site 5.07 East Blean National Nature Reserve

### Location (car park TR194644)

East Blean is just east of the A291 Canterbury Road running between Sturry and Herne Bay. The car park is off the minor road signposted Hicks Forstal off the A291 and running towards Hoath.

### Management

The wood is a National Nature Reserve managed by the Kent Wildlife Trust.

### Opening times and access

The wood is open at all times. There is a height barrier to the car park.

### Birdwatching tips

Park in the car park and follow the trails. A good area of mature woodland is reached by following the public footpath running northwards to the edge of the wood. This is the best area for Lesser Spotted Woodpecker.

### Non-bird interest

Heath Fritillary butterflies in June and spring flowers.

### Warning

The paths can be very sticky in winter and after rain.

## 5.08 Larkeyvalley Wood

This small woodland is a mixture of high forest, mainly of beech trees, and coppiced woodland. Fallen trees from the 1987 storm add interest and atmosphere.

### Birds

Year round: common woodland birds including Lesser Spotted Woodpecker and Marsh Tit.

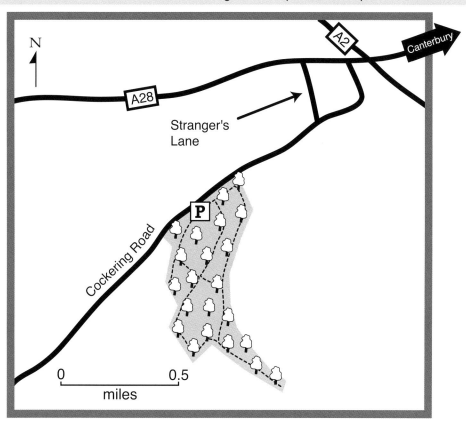

## Site 5.08 Larkeyvalley Wood

### Location (car park TR125557)

This wood is just south-west of Canterbury off the Cockering Road, which is accessible from the A28 adjacent to where it joins the A2.

### Management

The wood is a Site of Special Scientific Interest and Local Nature Reserve and is managed by Canterbury City Council.

### Opening times and access

The wood is open at all times. There are buses to Thanington.

### Other amenities

There are shops, places to eat and a petrol station along the A28 to Canterbury.

### Birdwatching tips

Walk any of the well maintained paths and rides. The northern section of the wood has the best areas of mature woodland whilst the southern section has more coppiced areas.

### Warning

Do not leave valuables visible in your car.

## 5.09 Park and West Woods, Lyminge Forest

This forest contains very few mature deciduous trees but many mature spruce and fir trees among the younger conifers. Clusters of mature conifers are home to small numbers of breeding Firecrests. Spring is the best time to listen out for their distinctive song amongst the many Goldcrests that breed here.

### Birds
Year round: woodland species, Willow Tit
Spring and summer: Turtle Dove, Firecrest, Nightjar, Nightingale, warblers.

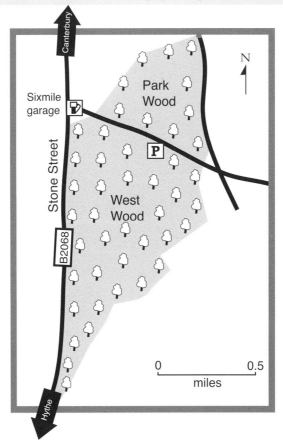

86

## Site 5.09 Park and West Woods, Lyminge Forest

### Location (car park TR142439)
The car park is situated on the minor road that runs off the B2068 between Hythe and Canterbury at Sixmile garage. Park Wood lies to the north of the car park, just across the road, and West Wood lies to the south.

### Management
Managed by the Forestry Commission for conservation, amenity and timber production.

### Opening times and access
Open at all times. There is a height barrier to the car park.

### Other amenities
There is a non-24 h garage at the B2068 junction and several pubs locally.

### Birdwatching tips
The woods are small with well maintained rides and paths. Explore both thoroughly.

## 5.10 King's Wood, Challock

This is a large and varied family-friendly woodland, enlivened by sculptures and easily accessible along several well maintained trails. It is a curiously confusing wood to navigate, with far more trails and paths then are marked on any maps. Nightjars are a little further into the forest than some other sites but this wood is excellent for winter birds and a good place to watch for raptors.

### Birds
Year round: Tawny Owl, Woodcock
Spring and summer: Tree Pipit, Nightjar, Turtle Dove, Nightingale, warblers
Autumn, winter and spring: Common Crossbill, Lesser Redpoll, Siskin, Brambling.

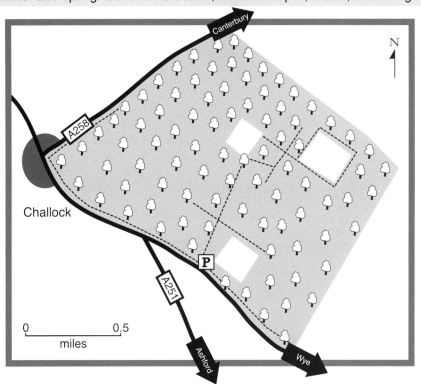

## Site 5.10 King's Wood, Challock

### Location (car park TR024499)
The wood lies on the downs between Ashford and Canterbury on the west side of the Stour River. The car park is off the minor road between Challock and Wye to the west of the A28. There is a railway station at Wye 2.5 miles away.

### Management
Kings Wood is managed by the Forestry Commission for commercial use, access and conservation.

### Opening times and access
The car park and wood are open and accessible at all times. There are occasional restrictions for special events. The car park has a height barrier.

### Other amenities
Children can climb on the sculptures. There are information boards and a map near the car park.

## Birdwatching tips

From the main car park, there are numerous rides and paths through the wood. A simple route that takes you to two open areas where Tree Pipit, Woodcock and Nightjar are present in the summer is to follow the main footpath straight ahead across the cleared area, downhill through the sweet chestnut and across the first ride climbing into the mature beech and larch forest, which can also be good for wintering species. The path eventually comes to a junction. Immediately on your left is the first open area, which is good for Nightjar. Either watch from the edge of the forest and return to the car park by the same route or turn left and follow the path across the clearing. At the end, turn right along the edge of the clearing back into the wood going downhill and across the ride at the bottom. Climb through the wood on the path and there is an area of sweet chestnut coppice on your left. This open area holds Tree Pipit, Nightjar and Woodcock. It is also a good area from where to scan the sky for raptors and other birds flying over the canopy. Alternatively, when you reach the first ride, instead of going straight across, turn left and then right bringing you to a junction at the edge of the first cleared area. Several routes take you back to the car park from here. A third open area is close to the car park.

## Non-bird interest

Fallow Deer are present and can often be seen at dusk.

**Heath Fritillary butterfly**

# CHAPTER 6 Medway and the Weald

## Introduction

The Weald of Kent conjures up images of rolling wooded countryside, orchards and hop fields and, despite much agricultural change, urban growth and infrastructure development, this is still the case for much of west and central Kent. Stretching from the M25 to the edge of Romney Marsh, this area attracts less attention than the well known coastal areas of the county that attract migrants, raptors and thousands of wintering birds, yet there are several accessible sites in the area where interesting birds can be seen throughout the year. The wetlands created by the aggregates, extraction and water supply industries form the focus of attention for the birdwatcher, but close by are a variety of woodlands where you might find some of the increasingly difficult birds in the county.

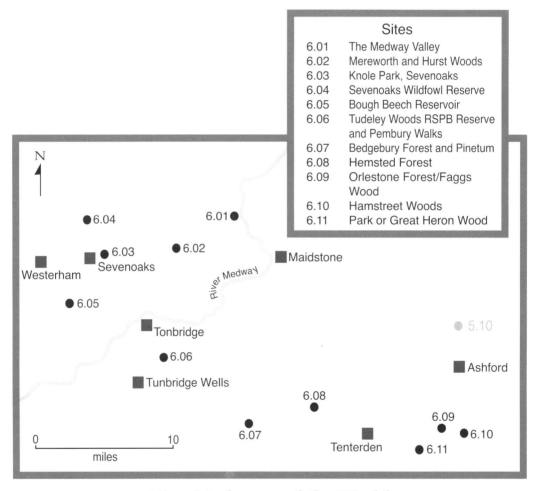

| Sites | |
|---|---|
| 6.01 | The Medway Valley |
| 6.02 | Mereworth and Hurst Woods |
| 6.03 | Knole Park, Sevenoaks |
| 6.04 | Sevenoaks Wildfowl Reserve |
| 6.05 | Bough Beech Reservoir |
| 6.06 | Tudeley Woods RSPB Reserve and Pembury Walks |
| 6.07 | Bedgebury Forest and Pinetum |
| 6.08 | Hemsted Forest |
| 6.09 | Orlestone Forest/Faggs Wood |
| 6.10 | Hamstreet Woods |
| 6.11 | Park or Great Heron Wood |

## Map: Medway and the Weald

## Special birds

Little Ringed Plover is the star breeding bird at the inland wetland sites such as Sevenoaks and Bough Beech. They are joined, especially at Bough Beech, by migrating gulls, terns and waders throughout the spring and autumn. Ospreys pass through on migration and occasionally stay for extended periods. In winter, Goldeneye, Goosander, Smew and Bittern regularly visit these areas, especially in the Medway Valley, where Cetti's Warbler is resident and joined in spring by Nightingale. Increasingly in Kent, the latter is a bird of damp scrubby habitats rather than dry woodland. Damper patches of woodland hold the last few pairs of the rapidly declining Willow Tit, whilst in better woodland, Marsh Tit and Lesser Spotted Woodpecker can be found amongst their more common relatives. The Hawfinch is another rapidly declining species but can still occasionally be found. Between September and April, Brambling, Siskin and Lesser Redpoll, and in some years Common Crossbill, are present throughout the area. In some of the more open park-like woodland, the declining Redstart clings on as a breeding species in the county and there are occasional signs that Woodlark might colonise. The enigmatic Nightjar is present at several sites, as is Woodcock. Hobbies gather around wetland sites, and slowly colonising the county are Common Buzzard, Goshawk and Honey Buzzard. Watch out for these species in this well-wooded part of the county and report any seen to the county recorder.

## Timing

Spring is an exciting time to visit with waves of migrants reaching their inland breeding grounds or passing through on their way north. A visit to either wetland or woodland at this time of year will be rewarding. Among the earliest arrivals is Little Ringed Plover in late March. By mid April most of the summer songbirds including Tree Pipit and Nightingale have joined resident species in the woodlands. Migrating winter visitors such as Common Crossbill, Lesser Redpoll and Siskin will often be singing at this time of year and a few stay on to breed. By late May, Nightjars will be churring in woodland clearings and can be heard through to early August. An evening visit for Nightjar at most sites will also reveal Woodcock and Tawny Owl. The first southward bound Green Sandpipers return in late June heralding the extended autumn passage. This is the time of year when the wetlands provide the focus for birdwatching. Migrating Ospreys join small parties of waders, terns and gulls, and by mid September the first wintering ducks arrive. Bittern has usually appeared by the end of October. In the woodlands, many of the resident birds flock together and are joined by wintering thrushes and finches and, in some years, Common Crossbill. A cold snap during the winter will often result in hard-weather movements of birds onto the wetlands including Smew and Goosander, and of more birds into the woodlands, making regular visits to any of these sites worthwhile.

## 6.01 The Medway Valley: New Hythe, Abbey Mead and Leybourne Lakes

Despite somewhat insalubrious surroundings, and under pressure from development, these gravel pits provide a lovely mosaic of habitats in a small area, and are an easily accessible place to hear and see Nightingales and Cetti's Warblers.

### Birds

Year round: Cetti's Warbler
Spring and early summer: Nightingale, warblers
Winter: wildfowl, including Goldeneye and Smew, Bittern, Kingfisher.

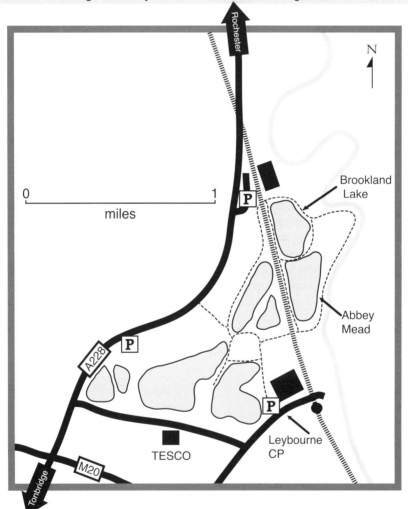

## Site 6.01 New Hythe, Abbey Mead and Leybourne Lakes

### Location (car parks TQ707615, TQ697603 (Brookland Lake) and Leybourne Country Park, TQ709599)

The lakes lie on the west side of the River Medway between Rochester and Maidstone and adjacent to the A228. The whole site can be accessed from any of the car parks.

## Management

Brookland and Abbey Meads Lakes are managed by Snodland Parish Council, and Abbey Meads Lake is a SSSI. Most of the rest of the area is part of Leybourne Country Park which is run by Tonbridge and Malling Council.

## Opening times and access

The area is open and accessible at all times.

## Other amenities

There is a cafe and toilets at the northern car park open reasonable hours from Monday to Friday in the winter and all week in the summer. There are places to eat in Snodland and a 24 h petrol station at the Tesco superstore at Lunsford.

## Birdwatching tips

The site is easily accessed by public and permissive footpaths, and is well used by fishermen and walkers. The lakes to the west of the railway line are worth looking at and there are areas of wet woodland. Nightingale and Grasshopper Warbler can be heard and sometimes seen close to the car park at TQ709599. Leaving the car park, follow the well made-up path bearing right and underneath the electricity wires to view the scrub. Cross the railway at the marked crossing and walk up the bank in front of you to scan Abbey Mead Lake. This is probably the best lake for wildfowl during the winter. Follow the path up the east side of the lake; Cetti's Warbler is resident in this area with good numbers of scrub and woodland birds, and Nightingale and scrub warblers are present in summer. The tidal reedbeds sometimes hold Water Rail and Bearded Tit in winter. Either cut back between Brookland and Abbey Mead Lakes or walk right round Brookland Lake. In the winter, scan any patch of reed carefully for Bittern. Cross back over the railway at the marked place and explore the lakes, perhaps choosing a different route back to the car park. Alternatively, park at TQ707615 and explore the area from the northern end. A visit in May with nine or even ten species of warbler and Nightingale singing, and the air heavy with the scent of hawthorn blossom is a must!

## Warning

Take care when crossing over the railway.

## 6.02 Mereworth and Hurst Woods

An area of mixed woodland with remnant beech woodland, areas of conifer, sweet chestnut and areas with remnant heath vegetation. It is a good site to see Nightjar and Woodcock.

### Birds

Year round: woodland birds including Lesser Spotted Woodpecker
Spring and winter: Common Crossbill
Summer: Nightjar, Woodcock, Tree Pipit.

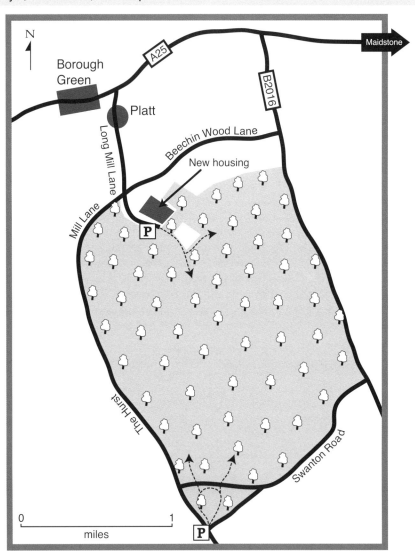

## Site 6.02 Mereworth and Hurst Woods

### Location (car parks TQ627559 and TQ631530)

This woodland is just west of Maidstone, close to the M26/M20 junction. To see Nightjars and Woodcocks, park at TQ627559 just south of Platt village, adjacent to a new housing development. Take Long Mill Lane south out of the village past the Blue Anchor Park and church. There is a turning on the left to the new development.

It is also possible to park at the lay-by adjacent to the National Trust viewing area at TQ631530 to explore the best bit of woodland.

## Management

The woodland is mostly privately owned and much of it is managed commercially. The small area around the car park is owned by the National Trust. A large part of the wood is a well signposted Ministry of Defence training area.

## Opening times and access

The wood is open at all times.

## Birdwatching tips

This is a large wood, much of it unexciting, although there is a good open area close to the parking area in the north of the wood where Woodcock and Nightjar can be seen on pleasant evenings between late May and August. Park carefully opposite the new housing development and walk straight ahead in the same direction as the road you arrived on. After a few hundred yards you have a good view over an open area to your left. Either wait and watch or you can easily walk fully around this open area on an established track.

Explore the rest of the wood from the northern parking area or from the National Trust viewing area in the south of the wood where there are some impressive beech trees.

## Warning

The training area is not a live firing range but heed all warning and advice signs anyway!

## 6.03 Knole Park, Sevenoaks

A deer park with some magnificent old trees that, shattered and broken, still show all the signs of the ravages of the great storm of 1987.

### Birds

Year round: common woodland species including Lesser Spotted Woodpecker
Spring and summer: Redstart, Tree Pipit, Stonechat.

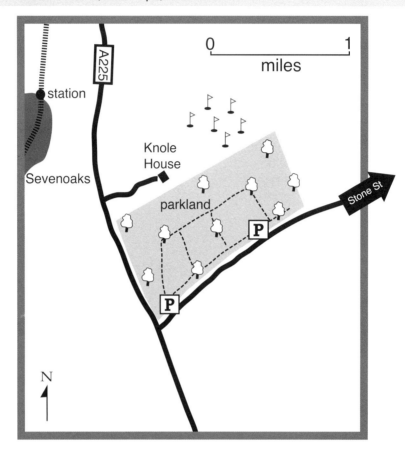

**Site 6.03 Knole Park, Sevenoaks**

### Location (car parks TQ540525 and TQ551534)

East of Sevenoaks, accessed from the minor road off the A225 that leads to Stone Street.

### Management

The park is privately owned and managed.

### Opening times and access

Open and accessible at all times. The nearest train station is at Sevenoaks just over 1 mile away. Buses stop close by.

### Other amenities

All amenities are available in nearby Sevenoaks

### Birdwatching tips

Redstart and Tree Pipit are present from April to August in the southern half of the park.

### Non-bird interest

A herd of Fallow Deer graze the Park.

## 6.04 Sevenoaks Wildlife Reserve

This gravel pit hosts a good variety of species, especially in winter.

### Birds

Year round: wildfowl, Lesser Spotted Woodpecker, Kingfisher
Spring: Little Ringed Plover, migrants
Autumn: Green and Common Sandpipers
Winter: Snipe, Water Rail, Lesser Redpoll, Siskin.

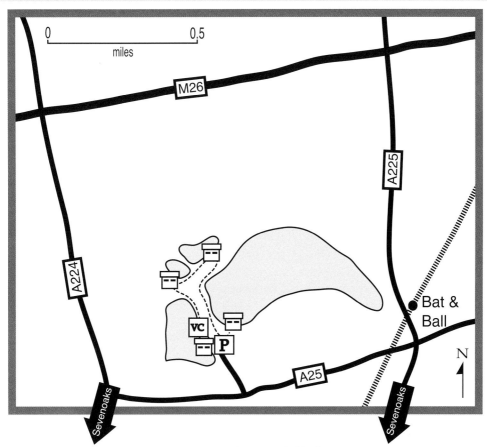

## Site 6.04 Sevenoaks Wildlife Reserve

### Location (car park TQ519566)

The reserve is on the north side of Sevenoaks next to the M26. Access is signposted from the A25.

### Management

The reserve is managed by the Kent WildlifeTrust.

### Opening times and access

Access to the reserve is free although donations are appreciated. It is open everyday during daylight hours. The visitor centre is open on Saturdays, Sundays and Bank Holidays between 10.00 and dusk. The Trust hopes to extend these opening hours soon. Call the Kent Wildlife Trust for details. The reserve is readily accessible by public transport. The nearest train stations, at Bat and Ball, Sevenoaks and Dunton Green, are all within 1 mile. Several bus routes pass close by.

## Other amenities

Toilets are available even when the centre is closed and there is a sightings board. All other amenities are available in Sevenoaks.

## Birdwatching tips

The trees and area around the car park are good and Lesser Spotted Woodpecker can be seen here. Walk the nature trail and scan the open water from the trail and hides. The alder and willow woodland can be good for interesting species such as Lesser Redpoll and Siskin.

## 6.05 Bough Beech Reservoir

This large man-made reservoir 5 miles west of Tonbridge is surrounded by woodland and farmland. There is a good variety of species to be seen at most times of the year.

### Birds

Year round: Mandarin Duck, common wildfowl
Spring: spring migrants, Little Ringed Plover
Autumn: Osprey, waders
Winter: wildfowl including Goosander.

## Management

The northern end of the reservoir is managed by the Kent Wildlife Trust as a Nature Reserve.

## Opening times and access

The visitor centre is only open from 11.00 to 16.30 on Wednesdays, Saturdays, Sundays and Bank Holidays between April and the end of October. The reserve may be viewed from the public road between the B2027 and Winkhurst Green (TQ496494). Park on the south side of the road only. A nature trail runs along part of the western side of the reserve from the visitor centre. The nearest train station is 2 miles away at Penshurst. There are bus services to within 2 miles via services 231 and 233 from Tunbridge Wells and Edenbridge to Bough Beech village.

## Other amenities

There is a sightings board when the visitor centre is closed. All other amenities in nearby villages or Sevenoaks.

## Birdwatching tips

Park on the south side of the minor road that divides the reservoir. Walk this road scanning both sides from here. The exposed margins in the smaller northern section are especially good for Little Ringed Plover in spring and summer, and many other waders in autumn. Mandarin Duck can often be seen among the overhanging trees. The open waters of the southern section are best for a range of wildfowl during the winter, including Goosander. A visit at any time of day can be productive with plenty of scrub warblers in spring and summer and in winter, finches and thrushes. Keep an eye out overhead for raptors such as Osprey in spring and autumn and Common Buzzard in winter. A public footpath, which gives greater access to areas of woodland and farmland, is signposted from the visitor centre.

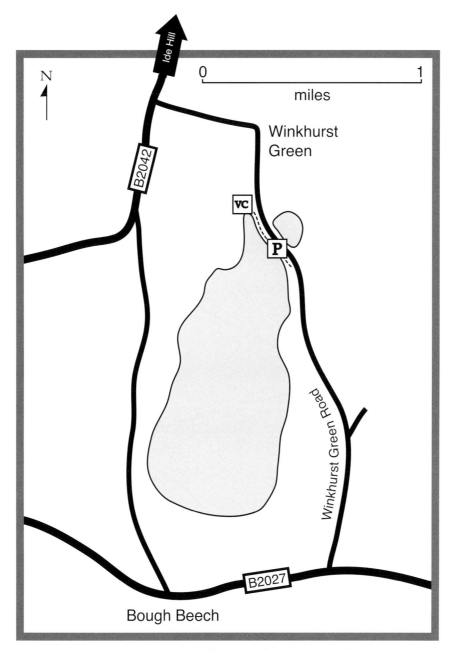

## Site 6.05 Bough Beech Reservoir

**Location (visitor centre TQ495494)**

The north end of Bough Beech Reservoir is 2 miles south of Ide Hill, Sevenoaks. The Reserve is signposted along minor roads from the B2042 and B2027.

## 6.06 Tudeley Woods RSPB Reserve and Pembury Walks

This varied wood in the heart of the Weald is an RSPB reserve, and gives good access to a wide range of woodland habitats and small areas of heathland known as the Pembury Walks.

### Birds

Year round: woodland birds including Marsh and Willow Tits (rare)
Spring and summer: Nightjar, Tree Pipit, Stonechat.

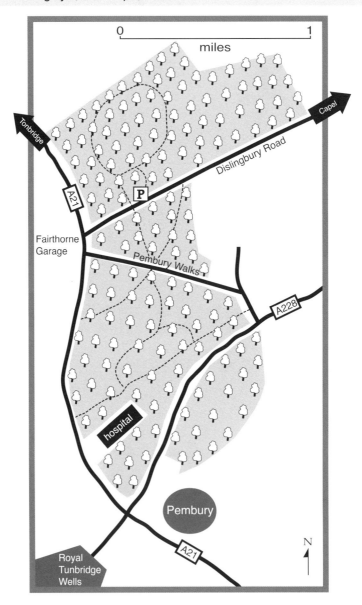

## Site 6.06 Tudeley Woods RSPB Reserve and Pembury Walks

### Location (car park TQ618434)

The reserve is between Tonbridge and Tunbridge Wells on the east side of the A21. The car park is off the minor road to Capel from the A21. Turn at the Fairthorne Garage.

## Management

The wood and heath are privately owned by the Hadlow Estate and managed as a reserve by the RSPB.

## Opening times and access

Open at all times (except Christmas Day). Several marked public and permissive paths and trails give access to the wood and heath and connect with long distance walks.

## Other amenities

There is an information board with a map and leaflets available in the car park. There are plenty of pubs around and all facilities in Tonbridge.

## Birdwatching tips

The best times of year to visit are the spring and summer. Park in the RSPB car park at TQ618434 and follow the trails heading south towards the heathland area. The woods are good for common woodland species including Marsh Tit and Lesser Spotted Woodpecker as well as warblers. Common Crossbill is often present and occasionally breeds. The damp valley areas where there are conifers are probably the last regular sites in the county to see Willow Tit. Knowing their call is essential. Nightjar and Tree Pipit can be found on the areas of heathland at the southern end of the reserve next to the A228. Occasionally Woodlark, Dartford Warbler and more frequently Stonechat are present in winter.

## Non-bird interest

This is a good wood for woodland plants and butterflies such as White Admiral and Silver-washed Fritillary.

## Warning

The trails can be muddy during the winter and after rain.

## 6.07 Bedgebury Forest and Pinetum

This large forest houses one of the largest collections of conifers in the world in the Pinetum, and makes for an extremely scenic area in which to watch woodland birds.

### Birds

Year round: common woodland birds including Lesser Spotted Woodpecker and Marsh Tit
Summer: Nightjar, Tree Pipit, Nightingale, Woodcock, Turtle Dove
Winter: finches including Lesser Redpoll, Siskin, Brambling, Common Crossbill and Hawfinch.

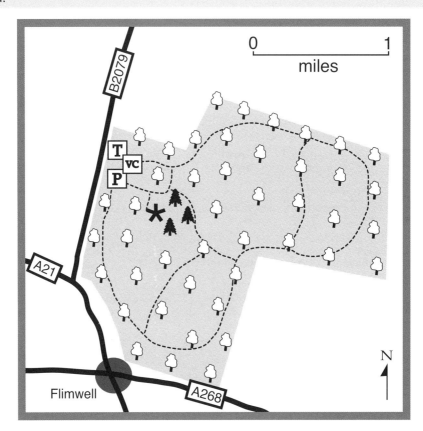

## Site 6.07 Bedgebury Forest and Pinetum

### Location (car park TQ715337)

Bedgebury Forest and Pinetum is just east of the A21 between Hastings and Royal Tunbridge Wells. The Pinetum car park is just off the B2079 which runs between the A21 and A262, between Flimwell and Goudhurst.

### Management

The Pinetum and woodland are managed by the Forestry Commission for conservation, amenity and timber production.

### Opening times and access

The Pinetum and car park are open between 10.00 and 16.00 in winter and 17.00 from March onwards every day. There is an entry charge to the Pinetum. A new visitor centre is planned.

### Other amenities

The shop, toilets and information centre are open daily and refreshments are available. A useful map is available on entry.

## Birdwatching tips

Bedgebury Forest is accessible at all times via the network of footpaths, trails and rides, and is home to breeding Nightjar, Nightingale, Tree Pipit and common woodland birds. The Pinetum in late winter is the easiest place in the county to see the now rare Hawfinch, as small numbers come in to roost then. Also present at this time are hundreds of commoner finches, together with variable numbers of Common Crossbill and Brambling. The Hawfinches often arrive a couple of hours before sunset and, especially on still winter days, sit at the tops of the conifers in the afternoon sun. A good place to stand is the "Fallen Tree". Either ask at the entrance kiosk for directions, or proceed as follows: from the car park walk straight towards the Pinetum, cross the small valley, after a couple of hundred yards, keep right and enter the area of huge conifers. The "Fallen Tree" is on your right. Just beyond is a sign that reads "Arbor vitae collection NCCPG". From here, look towards the cluster of Cypress trees slightly down the next hill. The Hawfinches will often be in the tops of these. As dusk approaches small flocks of finches stream into the Pinetum from the surrounding countryside to roost.

## Warning

It is easy to get lost in the main forest!

## 6.08 Hemsted Forest

This forest is easily accessible and is a superb place to watch Nightjars and Woodcocks. It is possible to hear and see these species without going far from your car.

### Birds

Spring and summer: Tree Pipit, Nightjar, Woodcock, Turtle Dove.

### Management

The wood is managed by the Forestry Commission for conservation, amenity and timber production.

### Opening times and access

The wood is open and accessible at all times. The nearest railway stations are at Staplehurst and Headcorn some 4 miles away.

### Other amenities

All amenities are in nearby Cranbrook. There are many pubs in the area.

### Birdwatching tips

The best sites for Nightjar and Woodcock are in the north of the wood. These are best accessed from four entrances along the minor road of Rogley Hill/Cranbrook Rd at TQ817371, TQ821370, TQ825367 and TQ832365. Park in the wide entrances, taking care not to block access, and walk into the forest. There are cleared areas within a few hundred yards of all four access points along this road where Nightjar and Woodcock can be seen. Tree Pipit frequents the cleared areas between mid April and July. Watch out for their distinctive song flight, and listen for their song throughout the day. Woodcock displays from April onwards but is most active and best appreciated on warmer evenings between May and July. Nightjars are present and calling between late May and early August. Arrive before dusk, stand at the edge of one of the clearings and wait.

103

## Site 6.08 Hemsted Forest

**Location (car parks TQ817371, TQ821370, TQ825367 and TQ832365)**
The Forest is between Tenterden and Cranbrook, just south of the A262. The best access for birdwatching is off the minor road that runs south of and parallel to the A262.

## 6.09 Orlestone Forest/Faggs Wood

An area of typical Kentish woodland between Ashford and Romney Marsh, with mature oak woodland, scrub and young trees, open rides and some conifers.

### Birds
Year round: woodland birds
Spring: Nightingale.

### Management
The wood is managed by the Forestry Commission for conservation, amenity and timber production.

### Opening times and access
The car park and trails are open at all times. Ham Street Railway Station is 1 mile away. The flat terrain makes this an ideal area to explore by bicycle.

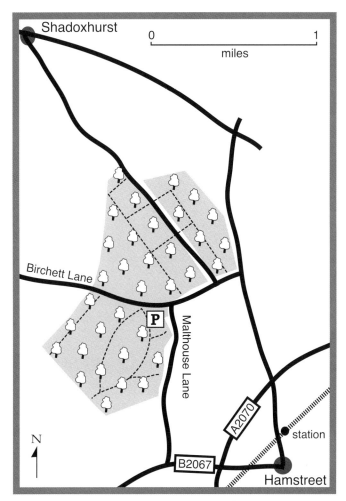

## Site 6.09 Orlestone Forest/Faggs Wood

### Location (car park TQ985348)

Just west of Ham Street and the main A2070 south of Ashford, quite close to site 6.10. The car park is at the junction between Birchett and Malthouse Lanes. The paths are well marked.

### Other amenities

There are pubs, shops and a daytime petrol station in Ham Street.

### Birdwatching tips

Park at the car park and picnic area and explore the area to the south and west using the trails and rides. The habitat is varied and includes conifers, coppice and mature deciduous woodland. Alternatively, park on any of the quiet public roads that cross the wood and walk. This is one of the best ways to hear Nightingale. Visit early in the morning or at dusk. For a real treat, visit after dark to experience the full power of Nightingales singing with little else to compete against. Either park in the car park, or simply stop and listen from any of the public roads around the wood. The rich varied song of the Nightingale carries several hundred yards. Evening visits will often be enlivened by Tawny Owl and Woodcock. Lesser Redpoll and other winter finches are often present well into April.

### Warning

Do not leave valuables visible in your car. The paths are very wet in places in winter.

## 6.10 Hamstreet Woods

This is a truly ancient woodland; a fantastically atmospheric place to explore several marked paths and trails and woodland rides.

### Birds

Year round: woodland birds
Spring: Nightingale
Winter: Common Crossbill, Lesser Redpoll, Siskin, Brambling.

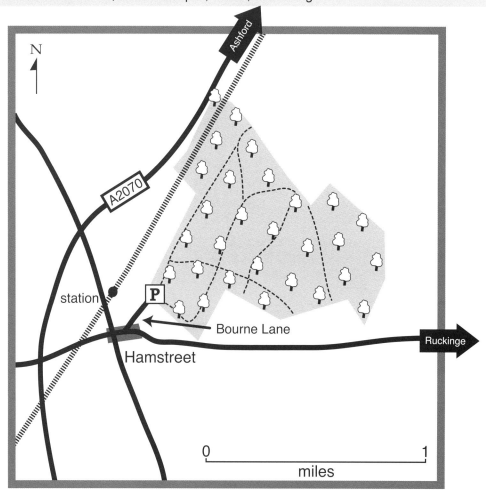

### Site 6.10 Hamstreet Woods

### Location (car park TR004338)

Just south of Ashford at the edge of Romney Marsh. The car park, which is not easy to find, is in Hamstreet village at the end of Bourne Lane. At the crossroads in the centre of the village follow the sign towards Ruckinge. Bourne Lane is then second on the left.

### Management

This is a National Nature Reserve owned and managed by English Nature.

### Opening times and access

The wood is open at all times. Two major walking routes—the Saxon Shore Way and the Greensand Way—pass through the wood. Hamstreet railway station is close by. Buses stop in Hamstreet village at the bottom of Bourne Lane. There is a recently installed easy-access trail in the wood suitable for wheelchairs.

### Other amenities
There is a map and information board near the car park entrance. There are pubs, local stores and a petrol station in Hamstreet.

### Birdwatching tips
A visit in late March or early April will be best for resident woodland species. From mid April until early June Nightingales sing in full force throughout the wood. By early May other summer visitors such as Blackcap, Garden Warbler and Willow Warbler are in full song. Like many woods, things are quieter from mid June until the autumn, when the flocking resident birds are joined by winter visitors. An evening visit in early May, enhanced by the scent of bluebells, is a wonderfully evocative experience. Arrive at sunset and listen as the evening chorus fades leaving just the Nightingales singing!

### Non-bird interest
The carpets of spring flowers from late March through to the end of May are beautiful.

### Warning
The paths can be very sticky and wet in winter.

## 6.11 Park or Great Heron Wood
This small well-managed wood is a typical Wealden woodland with a good variety of habitats in a small area.

### Birds
Year round: common woodland birds
Spring: Nightingale, woodland warblers.

### Management
The wood is managed by Kent County Council.

### Opening times and access
Open at all times. There is a height barrier on the car park. National Cycle Route 11 passes close by. Appledore is the nearest railway station.

### Other amenities
There is an information board in the car park. There are pubs, village shops, a petrol station and places to eat in Appledore.

### Birdwatching tips
Park at the car park and picnic area at TQ954317 and use any number of trails through the wood. Though not well marked, the wood is small and it is easy to find your way. The best areas are closest to the car park. A good birdwatching route is to take a trail out to the right of the car park and follow an anti-clockwise direction. The wet valley due east of the car park can be especially good for common woodland species. Nightingales sing throughout the wood from mid April to early June, but an evening visit in May is most productive. They can be heard throughout the wood in patches of dense scrub.

### Non-bird interest
An excellent wood for Bluebells.

### Warning
The paths can get very wet in winter.

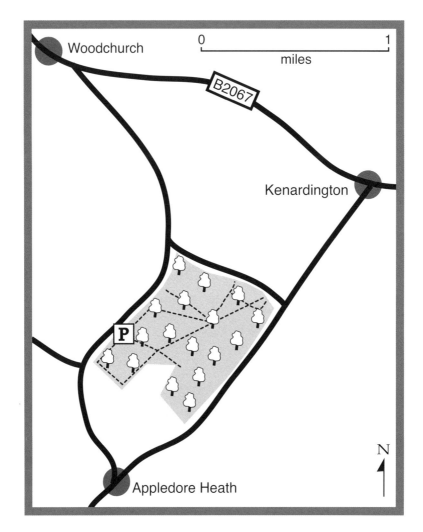

## Site 6.11 Park or Great Heron Wood

**Location (car park TQ954317)**

Just north of Appledore, off the minor road to Woodchurch.

**Nightingale**

## APPENDIX 1 Kent checklist

All species on the British Ornithologists' Union (BOU) British List in Categories A to C that have occurred in Kent up to the end of August 2005 are listed below. Also included are two widely recognised yellow-legged gull forms, Caspian Gull *Larus cachinnans* and Yellow-legged Gull *Larus michahellis*. We have also included Siberian Stonechat *Saxicola maurus*, which also seems likely to gain wide acceptance as a separate species. Another form not identified to species, Fea's/Zino's Petrel *Pterodroma feae/madeira* is also included. The sequence and nomenclature follows the BOU with some minor deviations to include more widely used English names.

**Anatidae (Ducks, Geese and Swans)**
..... Mute Swan *Cygnus olor*
..... Bewick's Swan *Cygnus columbianus*
..... Whooper Swan *Cygnus cygnus*
..... Bean Goose *Anser fabalis*
..... Pink-footed Goose *Anser brachyrhynchus*
..... Greater White-fronted Goose *Anser albifrons*
..... Lesser White-fronted Goose *Anser erythropus*
..... Greylag Goose *Anser anser*
..... Snow Goose *Anser caerulescens*
..... Canada Goose *Branta canadensis*
..... Barnacle Goose *Branta leucopsis*
..... Brent Goose *Branta bernicla*
..... Red-breasted Goose *Branta ruficollis*
..... Egyptian Goose *Alopochen aegyptiaca*
..... Shelduck *Tadorna tadorna*
..... Ruddy Shelduck *Tadorna ferruginea*
..... Mandarin Duck *Aix galericulata*
..... Wigeon *Anas penelope*
..... American Wigeon *Anas americana*
..... Gadwall *Anas strepera*
..... Eurasian Teal *Anas crecca*
..... Green-winged Teal *Anas carolinensis*
..... Mallard *Anas platyrhynchos*
..... American Black Duck *Anas rubripes*
..... Northern Pintail *Anas acuta*
..... Garganey *Anas querquedula*
..... Blue-winged Teal *Anas discors*
..... Northern Shoveler *Anas clypeata*
..... Red-crested Pochard *Netta rufina*
..... Canvasback *Aythya valisineria*
..... Pochard *Aythya ferina*
..... Ring-necked Duck *Aythya collaris*
..... Ferruginous Duck *Aythya nyroca*
..... Tufted Duck *Aythya fuligula*
..... Greater Scaup *Aythya marila*
..... Lesser Scaup *Aythya affinis*
..... Common Eider *Somateria mollissima*
..... King Eider *Somateria spectabilis*
..... Long-tailed Duck *Clangula hyemalis*

..... Common Scoter *Melanitta nigra*
..... Surf Scoter *Melanitta perspicillata*
..... Velvet Scoter *Melanitta (fusca) fusca*
..... Goldeneye *Bucephala clangula*
..... Smew *Mergellus albellus*
..... Red-breasted Merganser *Mergus serrator*
..... Goosander *Mergus merganser*
..... Ruddy Duck *Oxyura jamaicensis*
**Phasianidae (Pheasants and Partridges)**
..... Red-legged Partridge *Alectoris rufa*
..... Grey Partridge *Perdix perdix*
..... Common Quail *Coturnix coturnix*
..... Common Pheasant *Phasianus colchicus*
**Gaviidae (Divers)**
..... Red-throated Diver *Gavia stellata*
..... Black-throated Diver *Gavia arctica*
..... Great Northern Diver *Gavia immer*
..... Yellow-billed Diver *Gavia adamsii*
**Podicipedidae (Grebes)**
..... Pied-billed Grebe *Podilymbus podiceps*
..... Little Grebe *Tachybaptus ruficollis*
..... Great Crested Grebe *Podiceps cristatus*
..... Red-necked Grebe *Podiceps grisegena*
..... Slavonian Grebe *Podiceps auritus*
..... Black-necked Grebe *Podiceps nigricollis*
**Diomedeidae (Albatrosses)**
..... Black-browed Albatross *Thalassarche melanophris*
**Procellariidae (Shearwaters and Petrels)**
..... Northern Fulmar *Fulmarus glacialis*
..... Fea's/Zino Petrel *Pterodroma feae/madeira*
..... Cory's Shearwater *Calonectris diomedea*
..... Great Shearwater *Puffinus gravis*
..... Sooty Shearwater *Puffinus griseus*
..... Manx Shearwater *Puffinus puffinus*
..... Balearic Shearwater *Puffinus mauretanicus*
..... Little Shearwater *Puffinus assimilis*
**Hydrobatidae (Storm-petrels)**
..... European Storm-petrel *Hydrobates pelagicus*
..... Leach's Storm-petrel *Oceanodroma leucorhoa*

**Sulidae (Gannets)**
..... Northern Gannet *Morus bassanus*
**Phalacrocoracidae (Cormorants)**
..... Great Cormorant *Phalacrocorax carbo*
..... Shag *Phalacrocorax aristotelis*
**Ardeidae (Herons, Egrets, Bitterns)**
..... Bittern *Botaurus stellaris*
..... American Bittern *Botaurus lentiginosus*
..... Little Bittern *Ixobrychus minutus*
..... Night Heron *Nycticorax nycticorax*
..... Squacco Heron *Ardeola ralloides*
..... Cattle Egret *Bubulcus ibis*
..... Little Egret *Egretta garzetta*
..... Great Egret *Egretta alba*
..... Grey Heron *Ardea cinerea*
..... Purple Heron *Ardea purpurea*
**Ciconiidae (Storks)**
..... Black Stork *Ciconia nigra*
..... White Stork *Ciconia ciconia*
**Threskiornithidae (Ibises and Spoonbills)**
..... Glossy Ibis *Plegadis falcinellus*
..... Spoonbill *Platalea leucorodia*
**Accipitridae (Hawks, Eagles and Kites)**
..... European Honey Buzzard *Pernis apivorus*
..... Black Kite *Milvus migrans*
..... Red Kite *Milvus milvus*
..... White-tailed Eagle *Haliaeetus albicilla*
..... Eurasian Marsh Harrier *Circus aeruginosus*
..... Hen Harrier *Circus cyaneus*
..... Montagu's Harrier *Circus pygargus*
..... Pallid Harrier *Circus macrourus*
..... Northern Goshawk *Accipiter gentilis*
..... European Sparrowhawk *Accipiter nisus*
..... Common Buzzard *Buteo buteo*
..... Rough-legged Buzzard *Buteo lagopus*
**Pandionidae (Ospreys)**
..... Osprey *Pandion haliaetus*
**Falconidae (Falcons and Caracaras)**
..... Kestrel *Falco tinnunculus*
..... Lesser Kestrel *Falco naumanni*
..... Red-footed Falcon *Falco vespertinus*
..... Merlin *Falco columbarius*
..... Hobby *Falco subbuteo*
..... Gyr Falcon *Falco rusticolus*
..... Peregrine Falcon *Falco peregrinus*
**Rallidae (Rails, Gallinules and Coots)**
..... Water Rail *Rallus aquaticus*
..... Spotted Crake *Porzana porzana*
..... Little Crake *Porzana parva*
..... Baillon's Crake *Porzana pusilla*
..... Corncrake *Crex crex*
..... Common Moorhen *Gallinula chloropus*

..... Common Coot *Fulica atra*
..... American Coot *Fulica americana*
**Gruidae (Cranes)**
..... Common Crane *Grus grus*
**Otididae (Bustards)**
..... Little Bustard *Tetrax tetrax*
..... Great Bustard *Otus tarda*
**Haematopodidae (Oystercatchers)**
..... Oystercatcher *Haematopus ostralegus*
**Recurvirostridae (Avocets and Stilts)**
..... Black-winged Stilt *Himantopus himantopus*
..... Pied Avocet *Recurvirostra avosetta*
**Burhinidae (Thick-knees)**
..... Stone-curlew *Burhinus oedicnemus*
**Glareolidae (Pratincoles and Coursers)**
..... Cream-coloured Courser *Cursorius cursor*
..... Collared Pratincole *Glareola pratincola*
..... Oriental Pratincole *Glareola maldivarum*
..... Black-winged Pratincole *Glareola nordmanni*
**Charadriidae (Plovers and Lapwings)**
..... Little Ringed Plover *Charadrius dubius*
..... Ringed Plover *Charadrius hiaticula*
..... Kentish Plover *Charadrius alexandrinus*
..... Greater Sand Plover *Charadrius leschenaultii*
..... Dotterel *Charadrius morinellus*
..... American Golden Plover *Pluvialis dominica*
..... Pacific Golden Plover *Pluvialis fulva*
..... European Golden Plover *Pluvialis apricaria*
..... Grey Plover *Pluvialis squatarola*
..... Sociable Lapwing *Vanellus gregarius*
..... Lapwing *Vanellus vanellus*
**Scolopacidae (Sandpipers and Allies)**
..... Knot *Calidris canutus*
..... Sanderling *Calidris alba*
..... Semipalmated Sandpiper *Calidris pusilla*
..... Little Stint *Calidris minuta*
..... Temminck's Stint *Calidris temminckii*
..... Least Sandpiper *Calidris minutilla*
..... White-rumped Sandpiper *Calidris fuscicollis*
..... Baird's Sandpiper *Calidris bairdii*
..... Pectoral Sandpiper *Calidris melanotos*
..... Sharp-tailed Sandpiper *Calidris acuminata*
..... Curlew Sandpiper *Calidris ferruginea*
..... Stilt Sandpiper *Calidris himantopus*
..... Purple Sandpiper *Calidris maritima*
..... Dunlin *Calidris alpina*
..... Broad-billed Sandpiper *Limicola falcinellus*
..... Buff-breasted Sandpiper *Tryngites subruficollis*
..... Ruff *Philomachus pugnax*
..... Jack Snipe *Lymnocryptes minimus*
..... Common Snipe *Gallinago gallinago*
..... Great Snipe *Gallinago media*

111

..... Long-billed Dowitcher *Limnodromus scolopaceus*
..... Woodcock *Scolopax rusticola*
..... Black-tailed Godwit *Limosa limosa*
..... Bar-tailed Godwit *Limosa lapponica*
..... Whimbrel *Numenius phaeopus*
..... Curlew *Numenius arquata*
..... Spotted Redshank *Tringa erythropus*
..... Redshank *Tringa totanus*
..... Marsh Sandpiper *Tringa stagnatilis*
..... Greenshank *Tringa nebularia*
..... Greater Yellowlegs *Tringa melanoleuca*
..... Lesser Yellowlegs *Tringa flavipes*
..... Green Sandpiper *Tringa ochropus*
..... Wood Sandpiper *Tringa glareola*
..... Terek Sandpiper *Xenus cinereus*
..... Common Sandpiper *Actitis hypoleucos*
..... Spotted Sandpiper *Actitis macularius*
..... Ruddy Turnstone *Arenaria interpres*
..... Wilson's Phalarope *Steganopus tricolor*
..... Red-necked Phalarope *Phalaropus lobatus*
..... Grey Phalarope *Phalaropus fulicarius*

**Stercorariidae (Skuas and Jaegers)**
..... Pomarine Skua *Stercorarius pomarinus*
..... Arctic Skua *Stercorarius parasiticus*
..... Long-tailed Skua *Stercorarius longicaudus*
..... Great Skua *Stercorarius skua*

**Laridae (Gulls)**
..... Mediterranean Gull *Larus melanocephalus*
..... Laughing Gull *Larus atricilla*
..... Little Gull *Larus minutus*
..... Sabine's Gull *Larus sabini*
..... Bonaparte's Gull *Larus philadelphia*
..... Black-headed Gull *Larus ridibundus*
..... Slender-billed Gull *Larus genei*
..... Audouin's Gull *Larus audouinii*
..... Ring-billed Gull *Larus delawarensis*
..... Common Gull *Larus canus*
..... Lesser Black-backed Gull *Larus fuscus*
..... Herring Gull *Larus argentatus*
..... Caspian Gull *Larus cachinnans*
..... Yellow-legged Gull *Larus michahellis*
..... Iceland Gull *Larus glaucoides*
..... Glaucous Gull *Larus hyperboreus*
..... Great Black-backed Gull *Larus marinus*
..... Black-legged Kittiwake *Rissa tridactyla*
..... Ivory Gull *Pagophila eburnea*

**Sternidae (Terns)**
..... Gull-billed Tern *Sterna nilotica*
..... Royal Tern *Sterna maxima*
..... Lesser Crested Tern *Sterna bengalensis*
..... Caspian Tern *Sterna caspia*
..... Sandwich Tern *Sterna sandvicensis*

..... Roseate Tern *Sterna dougallii*
..... Common Tern *Sterna hirundo*
..... Arctic Tern *Sterna paradisaea*
..... Forster's Tern *Sterna forsteri*
..... Bridled Tern *Sterna anaethetus*
..... Sooty Tern *Sterna fuscata*
..... Little Tern *Sterna albifrons*
..... Whiskered Tern *Chlidonias hybridus*
..... Black Tern *Chlidonias niger*
..... White-winged Black Tern *Chlidonias leucopterus*

**Alcidae (Auks and Puffins)**
..... Guillemot *Uria aalge*
..... Razorbill *Alca torda*
..... Black Guillemot *Cepphus grylle*
..... Little Auk *Alle alle*
..... Puffin *Fratercula arctica*

**Pteroclidae (Sandgrouse)**
..... Pallas's Sandgrouse *Syrrhaptes paradoxus*

**Columbidae (Pigeons and Doves)**
..... Rock Dove *Columba livia*
..... Stock Dove *Columba oenas*
..... Common Wood Pigeon *Columba palumbus*
..... Eurasian Collared Dove *Streptopelia decaocto*
..... European Turtle Dove *Streptopelia turtur*

**Psittacidae (Parrots and Allies)**
..... Rose-ringed Parakeet *Psittacula krameri*

**Cuculidae (Cuckoos)**
..... Great Spotted Cuckoo *Clamator glandarius*
..... Common Cuckoo *Cuculus canorus*

**Tytonidae (Barn Owls)**
..... Barn Owl *Tyto alba*

**Strigidae (Typical Owls)**
..... Eurasian Scop's Owl *Otus scops*
..... Snowy Owl *Nyctea scandiaca*
..... Little Owl *Athene noctua*
..... Tawny Owl *Strix aluco*
..... Long-eared Owl *Asio otus*
..... Short-eared Owl *Asio flammeus*
..... Tengmalm's Owl *Aegolius funereus*

**Caprimulgidae (Nightjars and Allies)**
..... European Nightjar *Caprimulgus europaeus*

**Apodidae (Swifts)**
..... Common Swift *Apus apus*
..... Pallid Swift *Apus pallidus*
..... Alpine Swift *Apus melba*
..... White-throated Needletail *Hirundapus caudacutus*

**Alcedinidae (Kingfishers)**
..... Kingfisher *Alcedo atthis*

**Meropidae (Bee-eaters)**
..... Blue-cheeked Bee-eater *Merops persicus*
..... European Bee-eater *Merops apiaster*

**Coraciidae (Typical Rollers)**
..... European Roller *Coracias garrulus*
**Upupidae (Hoopoes)**
..... Hoopoe *Upupa epops*
**Picidae (Woodpeckers and Allies)**
..... Eurasian Wryneck *Jynx torquilla*
..... Green Woodpecker *Picus viridis*
..... Great Spotted Woodpecker *Dendrocopos major*
..... Lesser Spotted Woodpecker *Dendrocopos minor*
**Alaudidae (Larks)**
..... Greater Short-toed Lark *Calandrella brachydactyla*
..... Crested Lark *Galerida cristata*
..... Woodlark *Lullula arborea*
..... Skylark *Alauda arvensis*
..... Shore Lark *Eremophila alpestris*
**Hirundinidae (Swallows)**
..... Sand Martin *Riparia riparia*
..... Barn Swallow *Hirundo rustica*
..... Red-rumped Swallow *Hirundo daurica*
..... House Martin *Delichon urbicum*
**Motacillidae (Wagtails and Pipits)**
..... Richard's Pipit *Anthus novaeseelandiae*
..... Blyth's Pipit *Anthus godlewski*
..... Tawny Pipit *Anthus campestris*
..... Olive-backed Pipit *Anthus hodgsoni*
..... Tree Pipit *Anthus trivialis*
..... Meadow Pipit *Anthus pratensis*
..... Red-throated Pipit *Anthus cervinus*
..... Water Pipit *Anthus spinoletta*
..... Rock Pipit *Anthus petrosus*
..... Yellow Wagtail *Motacilla flava*
..... Citrine Wagtail *Motacilla citreola*
..... Grey Wagtail *Motacilla cinerea*
..... White / Pied Wagtail *Motacilla alba*
**Bombycillidae (Waxwings)**
..... Bohemian Waxwing *Bombycilla garrulus*
**Cinclidae (Dippers)**
..... White-throated Dipper *Cinclus cinclus*
**Troglodytidae (Wrens)**
..... Winter Wren *Troglodytes troglodytes*
**Prunellidae (Accentors)**
..... Hedge Accentor *Prunella modularis*
..... Alpine Accentor *Prunella collaris*
**Saxicoliidae (Old World Chats)**
..... Rufous-tailed Scrub Robin *Cercotrichas galactotes*
..... Robin *Erithacus rubecula*
..... Thrush Nightingale *Luscinia luscinia*
..... Common Nightingale *Luscinia megarhynchos*
..... Bluethroat *Luscinia svecica*
..... Red-flanked Bluetail *Tarsiger cyanurus*
..... Black Redstart *Phoenicurus ochruros*
..... Common Redstart *Phoenicurus phoenicurus*

..... Whinchat *Saxicola rubetra*
..... Stonechat *Saxicola torquata*
..... Siberian Stonechat *Saxicola maurus*
..... Isabelline Wheatear *Oenanthe isabellina*
..... Northern Wheatear *Oenanthe oenanthe*
..... Pied Wheatear *Oenanthe pleschanka*
..... Black-eared Wheatear *Oenanthe hispanica*
..... Desert Wheatear *Oenanthe deserti*
**Turdidae (Thrushes)**
..... Rufous-tailed Rock Thrush *Monticola saxatilis*
..... Ring Ouzel *Turdus torquatus*
..... Common Blackbird *Turdus merula*
..... Dark-throated Thrush *Turdus ruficollis*
..... Fieldfare *Turdus pilaris*
..... Song Thrush *Turdus philomelos*
..... Redwing *Turdus iliacus*
..... Mistle Thrush *Turdus viscivorus*
..... Swainson's Thrush *Catharus ustulatus*
**Sylviidae (Old World Warblers)**
..... Cetti's Warbler *Cettia cetti*
..... Common Grasshopper Warbler *Locustella naevia*
..... Savi's Warbler *Locustella luscinioides*
..... Aquatic Warbler *Acrocephalus paludicola*
..... Sedge Warbler *Acrocephalus schoenobaenus*
..... Paddyfield Warbler *Acrocephalus agricola*
..... Blyth's Reed Warbler *Acrocephalus dumetorum*
..... Marsh Warbler *Acrocephalus palustris*
..... Eurasian Reed Warbler *Acrocephalus scirpaceus*
..... Great Reed Warbler *Acrocephalus arundinaceus*
..... Olivaceous Warbler *Hippolais pallida/opaca*
..... Booted Warbler *Hippolais caligata*
..... Icterine Warbler *Hippolais icterina*
..... Melodious Warbler *Hippolais polyglotta*
..... Blackcap *Sylvia atricapilla*
..... Garden Warbler *Sylvia borin*
..... Barred Warbler *Sylvia nisoria*
..... Lesser Whitethroat *Sylvia curruca*
..... Asian Desert Warbler *Sylvia nana*
..... Common Whitethroat *Sylvia communis*
..... Dartford Warbler *Sylvia undata*
..... Subalpine Warbler *Sylvia cantillans*
..... Sardinian Warbler *Sylvia melanocephala*
..... Greenish Warbler *Phylloscopus trochiloides*
..... Arctic Warbler *Phylloscopus borealis*
..... Pallas's Warbler *Phylloscopus proregulus*
..... Yellow-browed Warbler *Phylloscopus inornatus*
..... Hume's Leaf Warbler *Phylloscopus humei*
..... Radde's Warbler *Phylloscopus schwarzi*
..... Dusky Warbler *Phylloscopus fuscatus*
..... Western Bonelli's Warbler *Phylloscopus bonelli*
..... Wood Warbler *Phylloscopus sibilatrix*
..... Chiffchaff *Phylloscopus collybita*

**113**

..... Iberian Chiffchaff *Phylloscopus brehmii*
..... Willow Warbler *Phylloscopus trochilus*

**Regulidae (Kinglets)**
..... Goldcrest *Regulus regulus*
..... Firecrest *Regulus ignicapillus*

**Muscicapidae (Old World Flycatchers)**
..... Spotted Flycatcher *Muscicapa striata*
..... Red-breasted Flycatcher *Ficedula parva*
..... Collared Flycatcher *Ficedula albicollis*
..... Pied Flycatcher *Ficedula hypoleuca*

**Panuridae (Parrotbills)**
..... Bearded Tit *Panurus biarmicus*

**Aegithalidae (Long-tailed Tits)**
..... Long-tailed Tit *Aegithalos caudatus*

**Paridae (Chickadees and Tits)**
..... Marsh Tit *Parus palustris*
..... Willow Tit *Parus montanus*
..... Coal Tit *Parus ater*
..... Blue Tit *Parus caeruleus*
..... Great Tit *Parus major*

**Sittidae (Nuthatches)**
..... Nuthatch *Sitta europaea*

**Certhiidae (Treecreepers)**
..... Eurasian Treecreeper *Certhia familiaris*
..... Short-toed Treecreeper *Certhia brachydactyla*

**Remizidae (Penduline Tits)**
..... Eurasian Penduline Tit *Remiz pendulinus*

**Oriolidae (Old World Orioles)**
..... Eurasian Golden Oriole *Oriolus oriolus*

**Laniidae (Shrikes)**
..... Isabelline Shrike *Lanius isabellinus*
..... Red-backed Shrike *Lanius collurio*
..... Lesser Grey Shrike *Lanius minor*
..... Great Grey Shrike *Lanius excubitor*
..... Southern Grey Shrike *Lanius meridionalis*
..... Woodchat Shrike *Lanius senator*

**Corvidae (Crows, Jays and Magpies)**
..... Eurasian Jay *Garrulus glandarius*
..... Black-billed Magpie *Pica pica*
..... Spotted Nutcracker *Nucifraga caryocatactes*
..... Red-billed Chough *Pyrrhocorax pyrrhocorax*
..... Eurasian Jackdaw *Corvus monedula*
..... Rook *Corvus frugilegus*
..... Carrion Crow *Corvus corone*
..... Hooded Crow *Corvus cornix*
..... Raven *Corvus corax*

**Sturnidae (Starlings)**
..... Starling *Sturnus vulgaris*
..... Rose-coloured Starling *Sturnus roseus*

**Passeridae (Old World Sparrows)**
..... House Sparrow *Passer domesticus*
..... Eurasian Tree Sparrow *Passer montanus*

**Vireonidae (Vireos)**
..... Red-eyed Vireo *Vireo olivaceus*

**Fringillidae (Finches)**
..... Chaffinch *Fringilla coelebs*
..... Brambling *Fringilla montifringilla*
..... European Serin *Serinus serinus*
..... European Greenfinch *Carduelis chloris*
..... European Goldfinch *Carduelis carduelis*
..... Eurasian Siskin *Carduelis spinus*
..... Common Linnet *Carduelis cannabina*
..... Twite *Carduelis flavirostris*
..... Lesser Redpoll *Carduelis cabaret*
..... Common Redpoll *Carduelis flammea*
..... Arctic Redpoll *Carduelis hornemanni*
..... Two-barred Crossbill *Loxia leucoptera*
..... Common Crossbill *Loxia curvirostra*
..... Parrot Crossbill *Loxia pytyopsittacus*
..... Trumpeter Finch *Bucanetes githagineus*
..... Common Rosefinch *Carpodacus erythrinus*
..... Pine Grosbeak *Pinicola enucleator*
..... Bullfinch *Pyrrhula pyrrhula*
..... Hawfinch *Coccothraustes coccothraustes*

**Parulidae (New World Warblers)**
..... Golden-winged Warbler *Vermivora chrysoptera*
..... Common Yellowthroat *Geothlypis trichas*

**Emberizidae (Buntings, Sparrows and Allies)**
..... Dark-eyed Junco *Junco hyemalis*
..... Lapland Bunting *Calcarius lapponicus*
..... Snow Bunting *Plectrophenax nivalis*
..... Yellowhammer *Emberiza citrinella*
..... Cirl Bunting *Emberiza cirlus*
..... Rock Bunting *Emberiza cia*
..... Ortolan Bunting *Emberiza hortulana*
..... Rustic Bunting *Emberiza rustica*
..... Little Bunting *Emberiza pusilla*
..... Yellow-breasted Bunting *Emberiza aureola*
..... Reed Bunting *Emberiza schoeniclus*
..... Black-headed Bunting *Emberiza melanocephala*
..... Corn Bunting *Emberiza calandra*

**Additional Species**
..... ...............................................................
..... ...............................................................
..... ...............................................................
..... ...............................................................
..... ...............................................................
..... ...............................................................
..... ...............................................................
..... ...............................................................
..... ...............................................................
..... ...............................................................

## APPENDIX 2  Useful addresses and contacts

### Kent Ornithological Society (KOS)

For details of membership contact:
KOS
c/o Dave Sutton
61 Alpha Road
Birchington
Kent CT7 9ED

The KOS website offers a great deal more information about birds and birdwatching in Kent, including details of how to join KOS and submit county records. This website also offers links to more websites covering birdwatching in the county.
www.kentos.org.uk

### Birdline South East

www.southeastbirdnews.co.uk

### The RSPB

RSPB South East Regional Office
2nd Floor
42 Frederick Place
Brighton
BN1 4EA
Tel. 01273 775333

For information on RSPB reserves in Kent visit www.rspb.org.uk

### RSPB Dungeness reserve

Boulderwall Farm
Dungeness Rd
Lydd
Kent
TN29 9PN
Tel. 01797 320588

### RSPB Blean Woods NNR

11 Garden Close
Rough Common
Canterbury
Kent
CT2 9BP

### RSPB Tudeley Woods reserve

12 The Grove
Crowborough
East Sussex
TN16 1NY

### RSPB North Kent reserves

For information on RSPB Reserves in North Kent including Northward Hill and Cliffe Pools contact:
Bromhey Farm
Eastborough
Cooling
Kent
ME3 8DS
Tel. 01634 222480

### RSPB Elmley reserve

Elmley
Sheerness
Kent
ME2 3RW
Tel. 01795 665969

### Kent Wildlife Trust

For information on Sevenoaks Wildlife Refuge, Bough Beech Reservoir and other KWT Reserves contact:
Kent Wildlife Trust
Tyland Barn
Sandling
Maidstone
ME14 3BD
www.kentwildlife.org.uk
Email info@kentwildlife.org.uk

### Dungeness Bird Observatory

11 RNSSS
Dungeness
Romney Marsh
Kent
www.dungenessbirdobs.org.uk
Email dungeness.obs@tinyonline.co.uk
Tel. 01797 321309

115

## Sandwich Bay Bird Observatory

Guilford Road
Sandwich Bay
Sandwich
Kent
CT 13 9PF
www.sbbo.co.uk
Email sbbot@talk21.com
Tel. 01304 617341

## English Nature Kent Team

The Countryside Management Centre
Coldharbour Farm
Wye
Ashford
Kent
TN25 5DB
www.english-nature.org.uk
Email kent@english-nature.org.uk
Tel. 01233 812525

## Forestry Commission

www.forestry.gov.uk

## Other

For information on Folkestone Warren and Samphire Hoe contact:

White Cliffs Countryside Project (WCCP)
Tel. 01304 241806

## Public transport

For public transport contact:
www.traveline.org.uk
Tel. 0870 6082608
The traveline website has links to other sites with details of public transport in and around Kent

Page numbers in **bold** for certain key bird species indicate the most highly recommended sites for finding that species.

A
Abbey Mead Lake 92
Allhallows 64
Alpine Accentor 32
Alpine Swift 34
American Golden Plover 45
American Wigeon 45, 61
Aquatic Warbler 48, 61
Arctic Redpoll 73
Arctic Skua 28
Arctic Tern 12
Arctic Warbler 40
Audouin's Gull 11
auks 12, 27, 36, 37, 39, 40, 43, 59, 65
Avocet 43, **44**, 48, 50, **51**, 55, 58, 59, **60**,
    62, **70**

B
Baillon's Crake 52, 73
Baird's Sandpiper 45
Balearic Shearwater 12
Bar-tailed Godwit 12, 14, 15, 48
Barn Owl 17, 19, 20, 43, 44, 50, 59, 60, 62, 76
Barred Warbler 40
Bean Goose 17, 18
Bearded Tit 4, **7**, 43, **51**, 53, 54, 55, 73, 74,
    **75**, **76**, 77, 79, 93
Bedgebury Forest 102
Bewick's Swan 4, **8**, 9, **19**, 20, 44, **50**, 70, 73
Bittern 4, 6, 7, 16, 17, 55, 73, 74, **75**, **76**, 77,
    78, 79, 90, 91, 92, 93
Black Brant 55
Black Kite 11, 23, 27, 34, 73
Black Redstart **11**, 22, 24, 25, 36
Black Stork 11, 45, 55
Black Tern **12**, 47, **48**, 51, 65, 67
Black-browed Albatross 12
Black-headed Bunting 51
Black-headed Gull 43, 67
Black-necked Grebe **7**, 67, 68
Black-tailed Godwit 43, **44**, **60**, **67**, 70, 74
Black-winged Pratincole 48
Black-winged Stilt 48, 62
Blackcap 73, 107
Blean 72
Blean Woods National Nature Reserve 81
Blue-winged Teal 65
Bluebell 107

Blyth's Pipit 54
Blyth's Reed Warbler 11
Bockhill Farm 31
Bonaparte's Gull 12, 45
Bonelli's Warbler 37, 66
Booted Warbler 30, 32, 37, 66
Bough Beech Reservoir 98
Brambling 73, 87, 91, **102**, 103, 106
Broad-billed Sandpiper 48, 61
Buff-breasted Sandpiper 61

C
Common Scoter 36
Canterbury 72
Canvasback 17, 61
Capel Fleet 50
Capel-le-Ferne 23
Caspian Gull 12
Caspian Tern 52
Cattle Egret 52
Cetti's Warbler **6**, 7, 73, 74, **75**, **76**, 77, **78**,
    79, 90, **92**, 93
chats 27, 32, 37, 39, 46, 47, 48, 65
Chiffchaff 11, 68, 73, 74, 79
Cliffe Pools 60
Collared Flycatcher 37
Common Buzzard 27, 28, 30, 37, 59, 62, 73,
    91, 98
Common Crossbill 73, 82, 87, 91, 94, 101,
    **102**, 103, 106
Common Rosefinch 41
Common Sandpiper 43, 59, 62, 70, 97
Common Scoter 12, 27, 47
Common Tern 12, 43, 59, 67
Common Yellowthroat 55
Conyer Creek 54
Copt Point 20
Cormorant 76
Corn Bunting 4, **17**, 18, **19**, 20, 32, 48, **50**,
    54, 55, 59, 62, 64
corvids **62**, 76
Country Code 3
Crane 51, 62
crows 62, 73, 74
Cuckoo 54
Curlew 15
Curlew Sandpiper 32, 34, 43, **44**, **48**, **51**, 52,
    55, 59, **60**, 70

**D**

Dark-bellied Brent Goose 12, 34, **39**, 40, **48**, **53**, 54, 55, **67**
Dartford Warbler 10, 11, 17, 101
Dengemarsh 8
Desert Wheatear 37, 40
divers 6, 7, 16, 17, 18, 32, 43, 54, 59, 61, 68
Dotterel 18, 27, 29, 30, 48
ducks 44, 60, 91
Dungeness 12
Dungeness Bird Observatory 10
Dungeness RSPB Reserve 6
Dunlin 15, 18
Dusky Warbler 11, 30, 34, 37, 40, 66

**E**

Early Spider Orchid 25
East & North-East Kent Coastline 26
East Blean National Nature Reserve 84
Eider 20, 21, 27, 32, 36, 37, 39, 47
Elmley National Nature Reserve 44
Emerald Damselfly 45
European Bee-eater 30, 52

**F**

Faggs Wood 104
Fallow Deer 88, 96
Fieldfare 54, 55, 60, 62, 73, 74, 76
finches 27, 32, 46, 65, 66, 74, 105
Firecrest **10**, 11, 22, 23, 27, **29**, **31**, 46, 73, 79, **86**
flycatchers 11, 27, 32, 37, 39, 40, 46, 47, 48, 65
Folkestone Warren 22
Fordwich 78
Fox 45
Fulmar 22, 24, 27, 29, 30, **31**, **36**
Funton Creek 70

**G**

Gannet 15, 20, 21, 27, 36, 37, 39, 43, 47, 48, 53, 59, 64, 65
Garden Warbler 73, 107
Garganey **6**, 43, **44**, 48, 50, **51**, 59, 60, 62, 64, 70, 73, 74, **75**, **76**, 77
geese 8, 80
Glaucous Gull **12**, 27, 61
Goldcrest 46
Golden Oriole 7, 73
Golden Plover **17**, 18, 27, **32**, 34, **48**, **50**, 53, **62**, 64, 77

Goldeneye 55, 58, 67, 90, 92
Goosander 90, 91, 98
Goshawk 91
Grasshopper Warbler 31, 67, 68, 74, **93**
Great Crested Grebe 12, 15, 37, 39, 41, 47, 48, 60, 64, 65
Great Grey Shrike 73
Great Heron Wood 107
Great Reed Warbler 45
Great Skua 28
Greater Yellowlegs 45, 65
Greatstone Beach 14
grebes 6, 7, 16, 17, 18, 54, 55, 58, 59, 61
Green Hairstreak 61
Green Sandpiper 19, 20, 43, 59, 62, 68, 74, 91, 97
Green-winged Teal 62
Greenish Warbler 30, 37, 40
Greenshank 34, 43, 48, **52**, 55, 59, 70
Grey Partridge 50
Grey Heron 59, 62
Grey Plover 15
Grey Wagtail 68, 79
Grove Ferry 76
Guillemot 12
Gull-billed Tern 65
gulls 14, 15, 16, 18, 34, 43, 76, 91

**H**

Hamstreet Woods 106
Hare 45
harriers 8, 79
Harty Marshes 50
Harvest Mouse 61
Hawfinch 58, **71**, 73, 91, **102**, 103
Heath Fritillary 82, 84
Hemsted Forest 103
Hen Harrier **6**, 9, 17, **19**, 20, 28, 30, 43, **44**, 47, **50**, 51, 53, 59, **60**, **62**, 70, 73, 74, 75, 76, 78
hirundines 11, 46, 65, 66, 76
Hobby **6**, 7, 27, 37, 39, 43, 44, 50, 51, 59, 60, 73, 74, **75**, 76, 77, **78**, 79, 91
Honey Buzzard 27, 28, 29, 30, 31, 73, 74, 91
Hoopoe 17
House Martin 24
Hume's Warbler 40

**I**

Iceland Gull **12**, 27, 61
Icterine Warbler 27, 34, 36, 40, 41, 46, 66

Isabelline Shrike 11, 34, 37
Isabelline Wheatear 23
Isle of Grain 65

**J**
Jack Snipe 32, 68
Jersey Cudweed 7

**K**
Kentish Plover 15, 32, 34
King's Wood, Challock 87
Kingfisher 54, 55, 79, 92, 97
Kingsdown 31
Kittiwake 12, 27, **29**, 30, 31, 43, 59, 64
Knole Park, Sevenoaks 96
Knot 14, 15

**L**
Lade Pit 16
Lapland Bunting 32, 39, 43, 48, 50, 53, 64, 65
Lapwing 18, 27, 32, 43, 50, 58, 59, 62, 64, 77
Larkeyvalley Wood 85
Leach's Petrel 43, 48, 52, 59, 65
Lesser Emperor 7
Lesser Grey Shrike 34
Lesser Redpoll 73, 76, 79, 82, 87, 91, 97,
    98, 102, 105, 106
Lesser Scaup 18
Lesser Spotted Woodpecker 73, **81**, 84, 85,
    91, 94, 96, **97**, 98, 101, 102
Lesser Whitethroat 74
Lesser Yellowlegs 45, 61
Leybourne Lake 92
Leysdown Coastal Park 47
Little Auk 37, 43, 59
Little Bittern 52, 73
Little Bunting 30, 34
Little Egret 20, **51**, 54, 59, **60**, **62**, 64, 67,
    68, **70**
Little Grebe 60
Little Gull **12**, 27, 37, 39, 47, 48, 51, 53, 65
Little Owl 19, 43, **44**, 45, 59
Little Ringed Plover 6, 73, 76, 77, 90, 91,
    97, 98, 99
Little Stint 17, 18, 32, 43, **44**, 48, **51**, 59,
    **60**, 70
Little Stour Valley 79
Little Tern 43, **48**, 51, 53, 54, 55, 59
Long-billed Dowitcher 52
Long-eared Owl 62
Long-tailed Duck 58, 61

Long-tailed Skua 12, 40
Lyminge Forest 86

**M**
Maid of Kent 45
Mandarin 98
Manx Shearwater 12, 37, 39, 47, 48
Marsh Harrier 6, 7, 17, 19, 20, 27, 28, 30,
    32, 37, 39, 43, **44**, 47, 48, **50**, **51**, 53,
    54, 59, 62, 64, 70, 73, 74, **75**, **76**,
    78, 79
Marsh Sandpiper 61, 62
Marsh Tit **71**, 73, **81**, 85, 91, **100**, 101, 102
Medicinal Leech 7
Mediterranean Gull 5, **14**, 15, **20**, 21, 27, 43,
    **44**, 45, 48, 50, 51, 67
Medway Estuary 58
Medway Valley 92
Mereworth and Hurst Woods 94
Merlin **8**, 9, 27, 28, 30, 43, **44**, 47, **50**, 51,
    53, 59, **60**, **62**, 70, 73, 76
migrants 10, 16, 17, 23, 29, 31, 32, 36, 37,
    39, 40, 41, 97, 98
Minnis Bay 37
Montagu's Harrier 27, 28, 43, 50, 51, 59
Murston 55

**N**
New Hythe Lake 92
Night Heron 17
Nightingale 20, 60, 62, 67, 73, 74, 75, 76,
    **81**, 82, 84, 86, 87, 91, **92**, 93, 102,
    103, 104, 105, **106**, 107
Nightjar 73, 74, 81, **82**, 86, 87, 88, 91, **94**,
    95, 100, 101, 102, **103**
North Foreland 36
Northdown Park 36
Northward Hill 62
Nutcracker 32

**O**
Oare Marshes Local Nature Reserve 51
Olive-backed Pipit 23
Oriental Pratincole 48
Orlestone Forest 104
Ortolan Bunting 27, 32, 40
Osprey 27, 28, 43, 51, 54, 55, 59, 73, 74,
    75, 76, 90, 91, 98
Oystercatcher 15, 43, 59, 67

**P**

Pacific Golden Plover 45
Paddyfield Warbler 54
Pallas's Warbler 11, 27, 30, 32, 34, 36, 37,
    46, 66
Pallid Harrier 45
Pallid Swift 11, 61
Park and West Woods 86
Park Wood 107
Pectoral Sandpiper 61, 77
Pembury Walks 100
Penduline Tit 5, 7
Peregrine 5, 6, 20, 21, 22, 23, 24, 25, 27,
    **29**, 30, 43, **44**, 45, 47, **50**, 59, 60, **62**,
    70, 73
petrels 12, 40
Pied Flycatcher 11, 27, 36, 66
Pied Wheatear 37, 40
pigeons 62, 73, 74
Pinetum 102
pipits 27, 46, 65, 66
Pochard 18, 74
Pomarine Skua 4, 12, 28, 40
Purple Heron 40, 73, 74
Purple Sandpiper 5, 22, **36**, 37

**R**

Radde's Warbler 30, 32, 34, 37
raptors 7, 27, 29, 31, 36, 43, 48
rarities 6, 10
Reculver 39
Red Kite 73
Red-backed Shrike 41, 43, 46, 59, 66
Red-breasted Flycatcher 27, 34, 40, 46
Red-breasted Goose 48, 55, 62
Red-breasted Merganser 21, 51, **54**, **55**, **67**
Red-eyed Damselfly 25
Red-flanked Bluetail 32
Red-footed Falcon 27, 34, 51, 73, 76
Red-legged Partridge 50
Red-necked Phalarope 61
Red-rumped Swallow 32
Red-throated Diver **12**, 27, **36**, 37, 39, 41,
    47, **48**, 53, 55, 64, 65
Red-veined Darter 7, 25
Redshank 43, 58, 59, 62, 64, 67
Redstart 11, 27, 36, 66, 73, 91, **96**
Redwing 54, 55, 60, 62, 73, 74, 76
Reed Warbler 51, 53, 67, 74
Richard's Pipit 37, 41
Ring Ouzel 22, 24, 27, 29, 31, 36, 37, 39
Riverside Country Park 67

Rock Pipit 22, 23, 24, 25, 27, **29**, 31, **36**
Rock Samphire 23
Rose-ringed Parakeet **36**, 37
Roseate Tern 12, 34
Rough-legged Buzzard 27, 28, 37, 43, 51
Ruff 18, 43, **44**, 50, **51**, 59, 60, 62, 74, 76, 77
Rustic Bunting 37

**S**

Sabine's Gull 12, 43, 59
Samphire Hoe 24
Sand Martin 43, 59, 74, 77
Sanderling **5**, 14, 15, **36**, 37
Sandwich Bay Field Centre & Bird Obs 32
Sandwich Tern 12, 59
Sardinian Warbler 11, 30, 34
Savi's Warbler 73, 75
Scarce Emerald Damselfly 45, 61
Scaup **16**, **17**, 55, 58, 61, 74
Scotney Pit 17
seabirds 20, 22, 24, 41, 43, 52, 59
seaduck 27, 48, 54, 68
Seasalter 53
Seaton Pits 79
Sedge Warbler 51, 53, 67, 74
Semipalmated Sandpiper 45
Serin 5, 11, 46
Sevenoaks Wildfowl Reserve 97
Shag 5, 20, 21, 22
Sharp-tailed Sandpiper 34, 45
shearwaters 27, 32, 36, 40, 65
Sheppey 42
Shore Lark 27, 39, 40, 43, 48
Short-eared Owl 28, 43, **44**, **50**, 53, 59,
    60, 62
Short-toed Lark 61
Short-toed Treecreeper 11
Shoveler 74
Shrill Carder 61
Silver-washed Fritillary 101
Siskin 73, 76, 79, 82, 87, 91, 97, 98, 102, 106
skuas **12**, 27, 32, 36, **37**, **39**, 43, 47, **48**, 52,
    53, 59, 64, 65, 66
Skylark 27
Slavonian Grebe 67, 68
Slender-billed Gull 12, 73
Small Blue 25
Small Red-eyed Damselfly 62
Smew 4, **6**, 7, 16, 17, 58, 74, 79, 90, 91, 92
Snipe 97
Snow Bunting 27, 32, 37, 39, 40, 41, 43, 48,
    53, 64, 65

Sociable Plover 54
Sooty Shearwater **12**, 37, 39, 43, 59
South Swale Local Nature Reserve 53
Sparrowhawk 27, 28, 30, 37, 79
Spoonbill 44, 45, 60, 61, 74, 75
Spotted Crake 74, **76**, 77
Spotted Flycatcher 73
Spotted Redshank 43, 44, 51, 58, 60, 67, 68
Squacco Heron 37
St Margaret's 29
Starling 62, 73
Stilt Sandpiper 61
Stodmarsh National Nature Reserve 75
Stonechat **10**, **22**, 24, 27, 29, 30, 50, 51, 60,
    74, **96**, 100, 101
Stour Valley 72
Subalpine Warbler 40
Surf Scoter 37
Swale Estuary 42
Swale National Nature Reserve 48
Swalecliffe 41

**T**
Tawny Owl 73, 87, 91, 105
Tawny Pipit 37
Teal 20, 74
Temminck's Stint 61, 77
Terek Sandpiper 48
terns 6, 12, 15, 16, 21, 27, 32, 34, 43, 53,
    54, 59, 64, 91
Thames Estuary 58
Thornden Wood 82
thrushes 27
Tree Pipit 73, 81, 82, 87, 88, 91, 94, 96,
    100, 101, 102, 103
Tree Sparrow 4, 18, **19**, 20, 62
Trosley Country Park 71
Tudeley Woods RSPB Reserve 100
Tufted Duck 74
Turnstone 14, 15
Turtle Dove 60, 67, 73, 82, 86, 87, 102, 103
Twite **32**, 44, 45, 48, 51

**W**
waders 6, 7, 32, 34, 43, 44, 45, 47, 48, 51,
    52, 53, 54, 55, 58, 59, 60, 61, 62, 64,
    65, 67, 68, 70, 76, 77, 91, 98
wagtails 27, 46, 65, 66

Walland Marsh 19
warblers 7, 11, 22, 27, 32, 37, 39, 40, 46,
    47, 48, 54, 55, 60, 65, 75, 78, 79, 82,
    86, 87, 92, 93, 101, 107
Warden Point 46
Water Pipit 74, **75**, **76**, 77
Water Rail 7, 54, 55, 68, 73, 74, **75**, **76**, 77,
    78, 79, 93, 97
Water Vole 45, 61
Westbere 78
Wheatear 10, 11, 22, 24, 43, 53, 54, 59, 62
Whimbrel 19, 20, 44, 48, 55
Whinchat 27, 50, 53, 54, 62, 66
White Admiral 101
White Stork 5, 20
White-billed Diver 12
White-fronted Goose **17**, 18, 43, 44, 48, **50**,
    51, 73
White-headed Duck 17
White-letter Hairstreak 62
White-rumped Sandpiper 45, 52, 61, 77
White-tailed Eagle 45, 51, 54
White-winged Black Tern 37, 48, 52
Whitethroat 74
Whooper Swan 4, 8, 9
Wigeon 20, 53
Wild Cabbage 23
wildfowl 6, 7, 16, 17, 18, 27, 43, 45, 51, 58,
    59, 60, 64, 65, 68, 70, 73, 75, 76, 77,
    78, 79, 92, 97, 98
Willow Tit 73, **86**, 91, 100, 101
Willow Warbler 73, 107
Wood Sandpiper 32, 59, 62, 70, 74
Wood Warbler 73
Woodchat Shrike 37, 40
Woodcock 73, 81, **82**, 87, 88, 91, **94**, 95,
    102, **103**, 105
Woodlark 91, 101
woodpeckers 73, 79
Wryneck 40, 43, 48

**Y**
Yantlet Creek 64
Yellow Wagtail 19, 20, 44, 48, 50, 62, 64,
    73, 74, 75, 76, 77
Yellow-browed Warbler 27, 30, 32, 34, 36,
    37, 40, 41, 43, 46, 59, 66
Yellow-legged Gull **12**, 59